HITLER'S

The c
of th

Also in Arrow by Rupert Butler

**THE BLACK ANGELS
GESTAPO
HAND OF STEEL
LEGIONS OF DEATH
CURSE OF THE DEATH'S HEAD**

HITLER'S YOUNG TIGERS

The chilling true story of the Hitler Youth

Rupert Butler

ARROW BOOKS

Arrow Books Limited
62-65 Chandos Place,
London WC2N 4NW

An imprint of Century Hutchinson Limited
London Melbourne Sydney Auckland
Johannesburg and agencies throughout
the world

First published 1986

Except where indicated, the photographs
are reproduced by courtesy of the
Historical Research Unit

Printed and bound in Great Britain by
Anchor Brendon Limited, Tiptree, Essex

ISBN 0 09 942450 9

ACKNOWLEDGEMENTS

In the preparation of this book I am greatly indebted, as always, to the staff of the Department of Printed Books at the Imperial War Museum, London, for its patience in supplying material and answering countless questions. Any writer on the Third Reich or the Hitler Youth finds the Institute of Contemporary History and the Wiener Library, London, of value, not just for its stock of books but microfilmed newspaper cuttings, British and German, going back to the earliest days of the Nazi Party. The Hans Tasiemka Archive, London, also supplied much useful material. I would like to thank Robin Cross for allowing me to draw on his book *V.E. Day* (Sidgwick & Jackson, 1985) for the chapters on Berlin at the end of the war. Debra Butcher provided useful translation from the German and my gratitude goes to Terry Charman, Vicky Clayton, Will Fowler, Andrew Mollo and Bruce Quarrie for research and editorial assistance.

'I want a youth, a cruel unflinching youth, as hard as steel – Krupp steel.'

Adolf Hitler in an address to Hitler Youth, Potsdam, 1936

Could be that the columns which halt here,
That these endless brown rows of men,
Are scattered in the wind, split up and dispersed
And will desert me. Could be, could be . . .

I shall remain faithful, even though deserted by all –
I shall carry the flag, staggering and alone.
My smiling lips may stammer mad words,
But the flag will only fall when I fall
And will be a shroud covering my corpse.

The words of Adolf Hitler converted into a poem by Hitler Youth leader Baldur von Schirach

1

Nuremberg, southern Germany, September 1933. A delirious cheering triumphant crowd surged into the vast magnificence of the Zeppelinwiese stadium, showplace of the ancient city.

They were celebrating what Adolf Hitler's devoted acolyte Rudolf Hess called the 'Congress of Victory'; barely nine months before the Nazis had swept to power.

And the day of this Nazi party rally belonged to youth – sixty thousand of them in red or black or white vests and shirts performing complex formation exercises for ninety extraordinary minutes, spelling out such slogans as 'Blood and Honour', 'Germany Awake' and 'Youth and Labour'.

They moved faultlessly round and across the arena, the words appearing in red and black and white, in circles and rectangles and squares. And always somewhere in the centre of the design was the dominant Swastika.

Overhead, the towers of Klieg lights supplemented the summer sun, and the forests of flagpoles surrounding the arena were draped with thousands of Nazi flags.

The show was swamped with music; a mixture of the bourgeois and the classical.

Every movement of the boys' *tour de force* was greeted with a tumult of applause, rising to a climax when, as a finale, sixty thousand polished steel knives were drawn as one and whipped head-high to simulate the effect of a blinding flash in the high afternoon sun.

For Nazi Germany, it seemed as if the day belonged to the young.

Munich, southern Germany, May 1945. 'The thousand-year Reich' of Adolf Hitler had become a charnel-house and its children were frightened, desperately frightened.

Their enemies should have been cowboys or Red Indians and their battleground a back garden instead of the blitzed, shattered streets of their home city.

Slung across Munich's Maximilian Bridge was a barricade of street cars, behind which fourteen-year-old boys in bulging, tattered, ill-fitting uniforms crouched in terror. They clutched, not toy pistols or bows and arrows, but Panzerfausts they could barely hold and were too frightened to fire.

But what made their bowels turn to water was the sight of the column of Sherman tanks rumbling towards them down the Maximilianstrasse.

This little knot of Hitler Youth – the Hitler Jugend – was fortunate. For these boys, the war was to end, not in a volley of tank gunfire but as prisoners of the Americans.

In Vienna, not all the Hitler Youth had been so lucky by May 1945.

Here eleven-year-olds, uselessly dangling machine guns and Lugers, manned anti-aircraft batteries while enemy bombers droned overhead, inevitably annihilating the puny defenders.

Hundreds of miles away, in a concrete cocoon fifty-five feet below ground, Adolf Hitler was preparing for the end in Berlin, where debris carpeted the streets, and a pall of dust crouched like some malignant curse.

This moonscape of craters and rubble had been subjected to merciless bombardment from American B-17s by day and RAF Mosquitoes by night.

The Fuehrer, abandoning at long last his military headquarters amid the gloomy, drooping pine forests of the Masurian Lakes, had returned on 16 January 1945 to the capital of the Reich. First he was in the now shattered Chancellery, but by the end of the month he had taken up refuge underground in a two-tiered concrete bunker with six-feet-thick walls divided into eighteen cramped low-ceilinged rooms.

From the airless claustrophobia of this concrete cave where night merged into day amid the baleful glare of electric bulbs, Hitler, the once formidable warlord who had enjoyed an empire stretching from the Atlantic to the Caucasus, celebrated his fifty-sixth birthday.

To visitors to the bunker, with its ghostly humming generators, fetid odour of boots and uniforms and acrid disinfectant, it seemed that the Fuehrer was a mere ghost at his own protracted funeral, rapidly advancing into a senility hastened by the reckless intake of barbiturates.

On his birthday, there was the final gathering of Nazi paladins – Speer, Bormann, Goebbels, Goering and Ribbentrop. There was no champagne, just protestations of loyalty and hollow optimism, fuelled by Hitler's proclaimed belief that the Russians would still suffer defeat in Berlin.

And there was something else, one last propaganda gesture which at least provided some employment for the Reich newsreel cameramen who still dogged the steps of their Fuehrer.

On his birthday and what was to be his last public appearance, Hitler left the bunker and made for the Chancellery gardens to inspect a line of troops.

This was, in fact, a pretentious description of a pathetic line of tired, beaten men and boys, consisting of tattered survivors of the SS Frundsberg Division, sweepings of a detachment from a beleaguered army group and, most pathetic of all, a platoon of Hitler Youth

3

troops. They were barely in their teens, all war orphans who had come to Berlin from Breslau or Dresden. The camera moved in to catch the Fuehrer tweaking one of the boy's cheeks in a forlorn and melancholy gesture.

Der Reichsschulungsbrief, issue No. 9, published in 1936, had said of Hitler Youth: 'Membership is open to all Aryans who are of pure-bred German stock, acceptance to membership usually being on 20 April each year.' And 20 April was the Fuehrer's birthday . . .

These were the children whom Hitler himself had robbed of childhood, whose older brothers believed in the Fuehrer's siren song which but a decade earlier had told them: 'Today, Germany belongs to us and tomorrow the whole world.'

And now thousands of their young bodies littered the streets of devastated cities. Even girls were not exempt. Earlier in the war, they had been thought incapable of loading a Luger pistol or a machine gun. It was different now.

No. 6 Battery of Flax Reserve Unit 61 at Vienna-Kagran was staffed almost entirely by girls. On one occasion they achieved the almost impossible: one of their 88-mm guns had shot down a Liberator bomber. But shortly afterwards the unit received a direct hit; three girls were killed and two wounded.

More than young humanity had perished; what had been annihilated was a vision of a generation. It had been born out of a myth which flourished long before Hitler – and on another battlefield, in another war.

2

General mobilisation in 1914 swept enthusiastic young Germans into the Great War with a frenzy of patriotic fervour. In the Reichstag, political parties buried their differences to cry for blood. Kaiser Wilhelm II, with his withered arm and imperial ambitions, proclaimed triumphantly: 'I see no parties any more, only Germans.'

Few men in the prime of life had the remotest idea what it would be like; for more than forty years no major power had been involved in a conflict of any size. It would, the generals and politicians asserted with confidence, be a swift affair of great marches and greater battles. Everyone would be home by Christmas.

Disillusion was not long in coming. By November 1914, the German advance on the western front for Paris had been halted at the Marne. To the Fourth Army the order went out: smash through the defensive line which had been established by the Allies between Ypres and the Channel.

There were few regular soldiers in the Fourth Army, which consisted largely of regiments of young volunteers, many of them students and schoolboys who, their last year at school remitted, had swarmed with enthusiasm to the colours.

Typical among them was Walter Flex, a fiercely patriotic schoolteacher's young son, who proclaimed: 'We need a tough, hard-headed national idealism that is prepared for every sacrifice.'

A disabled right arm spared Flex compulsory military service but did not stop him volunteering in August

1914. Now the youth who had been too weak to hold a duelling sabre would have to bear a rifle and be pressed into service with shovel and pick.

Impatient with the politicians and theorists of Wilhelmine Germany, middle-class young men such as Walter Flex believed that victory in the war would be seized by them and not by a bumbling older generation.

No political party, either left or right, seemed to have devotion to the national good. Flex said bitterly: 'I see only the two great economic interests, agriculture and industry, which fight each other in the name of conservatism and liberalism and exploit the idealism of the masses with patriotic or democratic phrases.'

The vacuum was filled by the sort of potent idealism which had led to the foundation of a German youth movement dedicated to freedom, the Wandervoegel – Birds of Passage. Flex recalled that a year before the outbreak of the Great War, on the centenary of the Battle of the Nations, in which Prussian, Austrian and German forces had decisively beaten Napoleon and driven him out of the country, Kaiser Wilhelm II had unveiled a monument at the scene of the fighting at Leipzig.

The event had been seen as a heaven-sent opportunity for members of the Wandervoegel and other leagues of youth, bound together under the banner of the Bundische Jugend, to mount a demonstration of their own.

On the evening of 11 October, groups of boys and girls, including Socialists and students from the nearby universities of Marburg, Goettingen and Jena, had converged upon a chosen site at the Hohe Meissner, a mountain south of Kassel wrapped in romantic legend. For here, according to ancient folklore, lived Frau Holle, legendary maker of snow.

Boys and girls had held their own Festival of Youth. Here a speaker had denounced 'the unfruitful patriotism which immerses itself in words and emotions'. Furthermore, 'The Free German Youth is determined to shape its own life, to be responsible to itself and guided by the innate feeling of truth. To defend this inner liberty they close their ranks.'

One speech was recalled later in sorrow and bitterness by Walter Flex.

Gustav Wyneken, a respected German educational reformer and ardent supporter of the German youth movement, had produced a fine flood of rhetoric: 'When I look at the glowing valleys of our fatherland spread out at our feet I can wish nothing other than that the day may never come on which we are compelled to carry war into the valleys of a foreign people . . . '

But now that day had come.

Scene of the Gethsemane of German youth was in Flanders at the village of Langemarck, where there was a heavily defended core within the British position.

The firepower of the Allied guns had scythed into the 26th Reserve Corps of the Fourth Army. The units were decimated; it became obvious that any further push would be criminally futile. But legend said that above the bloody chaos of battle an ardent young voice was heard singing the 'Deutschland Lied' – *'Deutschland, Deutschland ueber Alles'* – the nineteenth-century patriotic and nationalist song.

That sole voice, so went the story, was quickly taken up by other comrades and soon they were all singing under the unremitting slaughter of the English guns. In wave after wave they advanced, until the battlefield had claimed most of them and there were few signs of life beyond the doctors and the stretcher-bearers.

As witnesses affirmed later, the few survivors kept up their sweet sad song. But the day had been lost. The statistics were spelt out in blood and slaughter. Some fifteen thousand young volunteers had braved the guns; hardly one third survived.

Yet death had not triumphed utterly over the heroes

of Langemarck. True, bodies lay bruised and broken on the battlefield. But the steady, throbbing pulse of idealism remained. The aims and dreams of the Wandervoegel needed strength and renewal from those who were left behind. The torch was passed to those who would fashion the next generation of the youth movement.

But the fact remained that the young legions had marched blithely into the mouth of the guns in quest of a vision.

It had been dispelled on the bloody killing ground of Langemarck.

3

A feverish, electric tension coursed through the main German cities in the wake of the Armistice of 1918.

It was not simply that the country smarted under military defeat; the very structure of law and order seemed under siege. And there was something else. No Communist party had existed under the Kaiser's Second Reich. Though the germ of one had developed during the war, its members had been content to remain within the ranks of the Socialists.

All that was in the past. Two rabble-rousing leaders, Karl Liebknecht and Rosa Luxemburg, both of whom had spent the war in prison, now came out into the open with their Communist organisation, the Spartacist League. The Spartacists, named after the slave who led the rebellion against the Romans, had taken to the streets bent on revolution.

Against them were ranged the forces of the Right – a

phenomenon known as Freikorps. It was spawned from the generation which had survived the heady romanticism of the Wandervoegel and been tempered and hardened by the relentless slaughter of the trenches.

There was shame, too. Shame at surrender on the battlefield, shame of a home front widely believed to be degenerating into Bolshevism. In Berlin, posters and newspaper advertisements screamed of the Spartacist danger. Soldiers were urged to rise and join the Freikorps to 'prevent Germany from becoming the laughing stock of the earth'.

While the illegal armies of Freikorps spilled on to the streets, the Spartacists tightened their grip on Berlin. In their control were public utilities, transport and munitions factories. In desperation on 3 January 1919, former saddlemaker Friedrich Ebert, the moderate Socialist who headed the government, dismissed the chief of police because of his Spartacist sympathies.

For Liebknecht and Luxemburg it seemed a pretext from heaven. The call was on for a full-blooded workers' revolution. And on the streets they tumbled, twenty thousand workers, brandishing weapons and red flags. The fog and the cold and the damp were ignored; groups swarmed into the offices of the Social Democrat newspaper, *Vorwaerts*, and the Wolff Telegraph Agency. Ebert and his associates lurked inside the Chancellery while an angry mob bayed outside.

By the following morning, the rifles of the Reds were trained down the Unter den Linden while their lieutenants were entwined among the statuary of the Brandenburg Gate. The railway stations and the government printing offices were Spartacist trophies. The predicament of a government with its grip on but a handful of major buildings was dire indeed.

But for the youths of the Freikorps it could have meant total defeat. Within a week, units from outside the city marched in and crushed the Red centres of resistance. The Spartacist leaders Karl Liebknecht and 'Red Rosa' Luxemburg had gone into hiding.

Freikorps General Maercker stormed: 'The threat is dire. Rosa Luxemburg is a she-devil and Liebknecht the type who will stop at nothing.' Eventually the couple were arrested at the apartment of a friend and hustled under heavy armed guard to Freikorps headquarters at the Eden Hotel.

Instructions were terse. Ostensibly, the couple were to be delivered to the Moabit prison and then shot 'attempting to escape'. No one could be sure there were not Spartacist infiltrators within the Freikorps movement; above all, the murders must be carried out quickly.

In the middle of the darkened Tiergarten, Liebknecht, already badly beaten about the head and body by rifle butts, was shoved from a car and shot by his escorts. For pint-sized 'Red Rosa' the end was more horrific. In a panic, her guards pumped a succession of bullets into the already half-dead woman a mere hundred yards from the Eden. Then the corpse was driven at high speed to the Landwehr Canal and flung in the water.

There was scant sympathy for the victims of the slaughter, who were dubbed 'Jewish agitators'. The *Vorwaerts* newspaper proclaimed:

> They were self-confessed instigators of civil war, murderers of the proletariat, fratricides, and their ears must ring forever with the fearful words: 'A fugitive and a vagabond shalt thou be in the earth.'

And what of the members of the Freikorps, some of whom had been the original Birds of Passage, so innocently tramping the countryside in an adaptation of a colourful Bavarian costume and who had been once so devoted to the revival of folk dancing and the beauties of nature?

Once they had sat around campfires singing the 'Song of the Freebooters', condemning parental religion that was largely sham. Politics, they had believed, were 'boastful and trivial, economics unscrupulous and deceitful, education stereotyped and lifeless, art trashy and sentimental'.

They had attacked the bourgeois trinity of school, home and church. With uncritical devotion they had dipped into the works of the philosopher Friedrich Nietzsche and Stefan George, the poet, who had cried: 'The people and supreme wisdom yearn for the Man! The deed! . . . '

In the politics of post-Wilhelmine Germany, shot through with the twin fevers of street violence and political agitation, the dangerously simple idealism of the Wandervoegel stood ripe for corruption.

As it turned out, the seeds were sown, not in Berlin, but far to the south in Bavaria.

Adolf Hitler was often to recall fondly his first visit to Munich. The day had been pleasant and sunny, the air washed by light winds from the Bavarian Alps.

In May 1913 Munich with its 600,000 inhabitants was, after Paris, just about the liveliest cultural centre in Europe. Hitler admitted readily that he had behaved like a wide-eyed schoolboy staring into a brightly coloured shop window. He had gaped enchanted at the grandeur of the statues, streets and buildings, and above all at the Koenigsplatz with its miraculous great arch, the Propylaen. He had been seized with a great and abiding love 'for this city more than for any other place that I knew, almost from the first hour of my sojourn there. A *German* city.'

But now, at the end of the war, it appeared to the

thirty-year-old friendless Austrian, the former Gefreiter – lance-corporal – of the trenches, to be a nameless place on another planet.

The scourge of revolution had coursed south from Berlin. Violence had erupted in Munich. The Wittelsbach King, Ludwig, like the Kaiser, had abdicated. Bavaria was in the hands of the Social Democrats, who had set up a Bavarian 'People's State' under popular Berlin-born Kurt Eisner. With his black, floppy hat and flowing locks he was the very epitome of a cartoonist's bomb-throwing Bolshevik.

Eisner had seized power without a shot being fired. Certainly, trucks crammed with his followers had rattled through the city, disgorging to seize main railway stations and buildings. But no one had raised a finger. The worthy burghers of Munich had shrugged at waking up in a republic and promptly gone to sleep again. It was a singularly tame affair; it was not to remain so for long.

The Freikorps, with former Wandervoegel in its ranks who such a little time before had brought their hopes to the trenches, were prepared this time to take to the streets as bullyboys.

Ernst Junger, a young intellectual and poet, caught the mood and was suitably intoxicated. He breathed: 'This is the new Man, the storm soldier, the élite of Middle Europe. A completely new race, cunning, strong and purposeful.' To Junger, they were not mere soldiers, but warriors for German salvation. 'New forms must be moulded with blood, and power must be seized with a hard fist.'

But, ironically, the abrupt end of Eisner's triumph was not to be the work of the Freikorps at all, but of an aristocratic nobleman, Count Anton Arco-Valley, who had served during the war in the Bavarian army. He had decided not to join the Freikorps, which he believed to be altogether too moderate in combating the Bolshevik threat and preparing for the new Germany.

Instead, Arco-Valley had thrown in his lot with the Thule Society, one of the numerous right-wing militant groups springing up at the time. Men like Rudolf Hess and Hitler's future party philosopher Alfred Rosenberg belonged; the group was virulently anti-Semitic and used a Swastika as its emblem, greeting each other with enthusiastic 'Heils'. Whether Arco-Valley had been ordered to kill Eisner or decided to prove the precise strength of his anti-Semitism has never been established; what is known is that at 9 a.m. on 21 February 1919, Count Arco-Valley came face-to-face with Kurt Eisner outside Munich's Foreign Ministry and fired two shots at him at point blank range. Eisner died instantly.

The workers erupted; a Soviet-style republic sprang into being. But not for long. On 1 May 1919, regular army troops dispatched from Berlin and local Bavarian Freikorps volunteers entered Munich and smashed the Communist regime. By 3 May Munich was secured but the cost had been sixty-eight young Freikorps lives. Plainly, this could not be allowed to go unavenged. Thirty Catholic workers of the St Joseph Society were seized at a tavern while making plans to put on a play. They were dragged to the cellar of the Wittelsbach Palace; twenty-one were shot or bayoneted to death under the justification of being 'dangerous Reds'. Power was shifting to the Right; but pernicious Left-wing influence was not to be ousted for another year. For Adolf Hitler, *his* beloved Munich had become a sadly repellent place.

4

The nondescript, untidy fanatic in the worn, ill-fitting blue suit edged his way confidently into the cellar room of Munich's Hofbrauhaus on 24 February 1920.

If Adolf Hitler was surprised at the strength of his audience – later estimated to be around two thousand – he gave no sign. Admittedly, pre-publicity had been extensive; leaflets and posters printed in bright red had been plastered all over Munich. The city had also been flooded with leaflets and slogans, but for the infant and almost laughably insignificant German Workers' Party, which Hitler had joined a year before, the holding of successful mass meetings was still something of a gamble.

Hitler was by no means speaking to the converted. Most of his audience consisted of Communists or Independent Socialists. The true idealists would have to be wooed by the powers of persuasion of a still fledgling orator.

Hitler had not been booked as the star of the evening. With ill-concealed impatience, he listened to the main address of an experienced speaker named Johannes Dingfelder, who attacked Jews and Bolsheviks with an anodyne delicacy that Hitler found infuriating, larded as it was with copious quotations from Shakespeare and Schiller.

Even the Communists appeared to take scant offence; more seriously, the bookish Dingfelder was in danger of boring the audience. Hitler sensed that unless he made an immediate impact the evening was lost.

He began with sweet reasonableness, outlining the postwar revolutions that had swept through Germany. Passion crept into his voice. Then came the flashing of the eyes, the extravagant gestures which were to become so familiar.

Hitler acted like a match to a powder keg. Suddenly, the room erupted with a volley of beer mugs and abuse from opponents who climbed on the tables and chairs.

The supporters were not simply in the Hofbrauhaus – they were in the corridors outside, waiting and eager for trouble.

The young toughs, creamed-off members of the Freikorps, supplied liberally with rubber truncheons and riding whips, poured into the cellar, ushering the hecklers outside so that their skulls could be smashed in comfortable leisure.

Almost as if opposition and tumult had not existed, Hitler continued his hoarse tirade. Above all it was an attack on the Jews, activated by what he had seen on the streets of Munich. Everywhere, he screamed, Jews were in power – Eisner and his successors in Munich, Liebknecht and Luxemburg in Berlin – their activities orchestrated by the Jewish press.

As if on cue, his supporters yelled: 'Down with the Jewish press.'

But it had not been intended that the evening should merely be an excuse for abuse and brutality. Hitler was shrewd enough to realise that his audience required something more.

A bright new dawn must be in prospect for the German people, one in which all, save the Jews, could share.

There must be a union of all Germans in a greater Reich. There must be colonies for excess population. Above all, there must be revocation of the hated Versailles Treaty which, following the Armistice, had forced Germany to accept the surrender of all her colonies, demilitarisation of the Rhineland for fifteen years, the payment of heavy reparations and the drastic trimming of the armed forces.

Hitler went further. He envisaged abolition of all unearned income, confiscation of war profits and expropriation of land without compensation. It was a shrewd pot-pourri of nationalism and socialism, a broad political programme of something for everyone.

The speech lasted a full two and a half hours. The final applause was so deafening that one witness, twenty-year-old law student Hans Frank, declared: 'If anyone could master the fate of Germany, Hitler was that man.'

Hitler, the success of the evening, was to put it in more florid terms: 'When I closed this meeting, I was not alone in thinking that now a wolf had been born, destined to burst in upon the herd of seducers of the people.'

How had it been possible? How had the former down-and-out tramp in Vienna, the unknown soldier of World War I, the derelict of Munich in these first grim post-war years, scaled so triumphantly the first rungs of the long, greasy ladder to political power?

The answer lay in a chance order given to the soldier Adolf Hitler in September 1919.

Before his discharge, Hitler had attended one of the soldiers' indoctrination classes with which the Reichswehr corps supplemented its armed combat of Left-wing subversion. He had shown promise and, above all, fervour.

One day, according to his own account, he had listened to a lecture which was less than virulent against the hated Jews. It had been too much; predictably, Hitler had launched into one of his familiar anti-Semitic tirades. His superior officers were impressed, particularly a certain Major Hiertl, who encouraged him to attend one group that was specially worrying the army. This was the German Workers' Party, a somewhat pretentious name for what was little more than a disgruntled talking shop of beer-swilling nationalists long on middle-class sympathies but short on political maturity.

With mounting frustration, Hitler sat through one of the group's meetings of twenty-five people gathered in a murky room of the Sterneckerbrau beer cellar. He later related: 'Everywhere these organisations sprang out of the ground, only to vanish silently after a time. I judged the German Workers' Party no differently.'

Later study of the party programme, however, led Hitler to change his mind. A pamphlet, *My Political Awakening*, written by a sickly, bespectacled locksmith named Anton Drexler, seemed to reflect many of his own ideas.

Events followed swiftly. Hitler found himself invited to join the German Workers' Party. He gave his reaction frankly in *Mein Kampf*: 'I didn't know whether to be angry or to burst out laughing. I had no intention of joining an existing party. I wanted to found one of my own.'

The party was nothing more than 'an absurd little organisation . . . club life of the worst manner and sort.' And yet might not the very obscurity of the party offer a unique chance for a young man full of energetic ideas? He wrote: 'After two days of agonised pondering and reflection, I finally came to the conclusion that I had to take this step. It was the most decisive resolve of my life.'

Thus Adolf Hitler became the seventh member of the committee of the German Workers' Party.

Hitler soon discovered that politics via rabble-rousing was all very well; by its very nature such a lurid bid for power and attention needed the backing of muscle and strong arms. On hand to supply these useful adjuncts was Hauptmann – Captain – Ernst Roehm, a thirty-six-year-old professional soldier who still held a commission in the army. Although not by birth a member of the

17

officer caste, Roehm had caught the admiring attention of the last Chief-of-Staff of the German Army, General Erich von Ludendorff.

Roehm was particularly useful because of his contacts in army circles; he had done much to increase the number of volunteers for the brownshirts, the SA – Sturmabteilung: storm-troopers. The able Roehm, a thick-necked homosexual, had joined the party before Hitler and saw in the SA the nucleus of a secret army which would eventually replace the Reichswehr. From it could be found a useful roster of out-and-out young thugs who relished laying about crowds and property with boots and rubber truncheons.

And yet one essential ingredient was missing if Hitler was to have a really effective power base. Its exact nature was sensed by one of those who had attended the tumultuous gathering at the Hofbrauhaus and who had subsequently listened to a number of other speeches, many delivered by Hitler on the steps of Munich's Feld-herrnhalle.

Virtually no one had heard of Gustav Adolf Lenk, an eighteen-year-old Munich piano-polisher who, during the revolutionary events in his home town during 1919, had joined the German National Youth Movement.

This particular group of clean-limbed young idealists had certainly not lacked fervour, but to Lenk it was far too middle-class ever to be even really effective.

In the summer of 1921, when Hitler assumed the leadership, the German Workers' Party had been renamed the Nationalsozialistische Deutsche Arbeiter Partei (the National Socialist German Workers' Party). Lenk had tried to join. However, at only eighteen he was precluded by the rules.

He persisted, pressing a useful friendship with Anton Drexler. But Drexler offered scant sympathy. Lenk was told: 'To build up this organisation is taking all the money and manpower we have. It would be far too

18

extravagant to take on a kindergarten. Besides, there are plenty of nationalist youth organisations. Eventually, we'll take over the lot.'

The furiously energetic Lenk was not to be put off so easily. He wrote directly to Hitler and deluged senior members of the NSDAP with memoranda. Eventually, Hitler, confident of his own security as leader, gave in.

On 25 February 1922, a circular was addressed to all sections and sub-sections of the NSDAP and the SA. It stated:

> Because of the increase of enquiries reaching the party leadership asking whether the movement has its own youth section, we have decided to call into existence the necessary organisation for the purpose of setting up a youth section . . .
> The organisation of the youth section will be conducted by the Sturmabteilung which will immediately work out in detail organisational statutes which upon their completion will be forwarded to the individual Ortsgruppen [local party districts].

Lenk noticed with considerable satisfaction that, once Hitler had decided to act, there was no question of delay. The circular was followed immediately by a public proclamation in the NSDAP's own newspaper the *Voelkischer Beobachter*. The issue of 18 March 1922 stated:

> The Party has now called into being a 'Youth League of the National Socialist Workers' Party' whose purpose is to gather all our young supporters who, because of their young age, cannot be accepted into the ranks of the storm-troopers.

The movement was to have its own statutes and would educate its members in National Socialist principles. The proclamation went on:

19

We demand that the National Socialist youth and all other young Germans, irrespective of class or occupation, aged between fourteen and eighteen years of age, whose hearts are affected by the suffering and hardships afflicting the Fatherland, and who later desire to join the ranks of the fighters against the Jewish enemy, the sole originator of our present shame and suffering, enter the Youth League of the NSDAP.

Then for those who cared to recognise it there was a clear hint that the party was looking forward to something far more ambitious:

We appeal also to youth organisations which at present are not part of any political movement, to join the German united front against the common enemy by joining us, thus creating a mighty battering ram.

Membership would be limited to 'Germans (Aryans) between the ages of fourteen and eighteen years. Foreigners and Jews cannot be members.'

Even so, Lenk recognised that it was a qualified triumph. Hitler was not prepared to concede everything: 'The organisation of the youth section will be conducted by the Sturmabteilung.' There could be no question of an independent organisation; any youth movement would be firmly controlled by the SA. Ultimate loyalty was to Adolf Hitler, the Fuehrer, and the party.

Lenk went on to be entrusted formally with the command of the Youth League. It was divided into two sections – one for those between fourteen and sixteen, the other for those between sixteen and eighteen. The second group was to be known as 'Jungsturm Adolf Hitler'.

Reservations apart, it did seem like a new dawn to the

'veterans' of the Wandervoegel. They were on their way; tomorrow, they believed, indisputably belonged to them.

Lenk's main asset to the new movement was not strength of personality or prowess as a speaker. He was a tireless and dynamic organiser – qualities which Hitler, still in the shadows as an obscure, rabble-rousing street politician, desperately needed.

He remained, however, wary of even the slightest hint of rivalry to his authority. Hitler was prepared to give the piano-polisher his head. But only up to a point.

Plainly, the young man had to be wooed; Hitler set out to do it through flattery.

On 28 January 1923, the first official Nazi Parteitag – Party Day – was held in Munich. It was a puny affair, when measured against later spectacular set pieces to be staged so magnificently by Hitler's Minister of Propaganda and Public Enlightenment, Dr Joseph Goebbels.

But the event was the source of delirious satisfaction to Gustav Adolf Lenk – which, of course, had been precisely Hitler's intention. The Jungsturm Adolf Hitler was given pride of place with a specially tailored ceremony. Bursting with pride, the baby-faced echelons received their own special pennants, garnished with an anchor and Swastika in the centre. Lenk received decidedly more than a pennant. Hitler personally assigned him the task of building up an administrative and organised centre for a Youth League throughout Germany.

On the surface, it was all very impressive. Small units sprung up in Nuremberg and outside Bavaria in such centres as Zeitz, Dresden and Hanau, as well as in the Dortmund area of the Ruhr. Lenk went further, extending his organisation beyond Germany, most notably in German Austria, where there was already a sister NSDAP organisation.

But overall membership remained small; by 1932, with the Weimar Republic in its death throes, it stood at 107,956.

Opposition to the Youth League was very real. Middle-class organisations regarded Lenk's members with hostility and in Catholic Bavaria the church, with its own youth groups, was not prepared to encourage poaching of members.

On the streets, however, opposition was to prove decidedly more vocal. Clashes continued in Munich, scene of the league's most tangible power base. In a series of running battles, the proudly displayed Swastika banners were seized by the police and smashed.

While members of the Youth League fought for their very existence on the streets of Munich, the brown-shirted members of the SA drilled in secret in the woods behind the Bavarian capital.

And in the seclusion of an imposing villa belonging to General Ludendorff at Ludwigshoehe, Hitler and a group of conspirators planned their next move.

It was to be momentous indeed. Events dictated that this would be nothing less than a march on Munich itself.

A new crisis was accelerating, prompted not by any events in Germany, but by the country's hated wartime victor, the French, architects of the detested Treaty of Versailles.

The blow which stunned an unwary Adolf Hitler and his followers was the charge by Premier Poincaré that the German government had failed to deliver 140,000 telegraph poles (part of the vast reparations payments) on time. France therefore intended to occupy the industrial heartlands of the Ruhr.

The news appalled the Nazis. Hitler saw the political initiative slipping away from him at a stroke. The French occupation served to unify the Germans behind the republican government, which the Fuehrer was dedicated to destroy.

The call of the government was for arms and the ruin of France. Hitler's protest was shrill and desperate: 'Our enemy is not France. Our enemy is the government and the traitors of 1918. We can deal with France later.'

As it turned out, there was no war. Instead, a campaign of passive resistance to the French was instituted by the government in Berlin.

Objection was swift and it came above all from Bavaria. The government announced its implacable opposition to knuckling under to the French in any way. On 26 September 1923, its members resigned, ushering into power as virtual dictator the royalist Ritter Gustav von Kahr.

His intentions were devastating for Adolf Hitler. Bavaria would secede from the rest of Germany; Prince Rupprecht, son of the exiled ex-King Ludwig, would be placed on the throne of a Kingdom of Southern Germany.

Something had to be done to prevent this upstart royalist from stealing the thunder of the National Socialists.

But what? The answer was provided by Kahr himself. He announced that his secession movement had secured the support of the local Reichswehr commander, General von Lossow, and the Bavarian police chief, Oberst von Seisser. The three would be addressing a meeting on 8 November in a vast beer hall on the south bank of the River Isar.

Hitler started to look with renewed interest at his legions of the SA, buttressed by loyal followers within the German Youth League.

Soon there would be urgent work for all of them.

5

Wilhelm Brueckner, commander of the SA Standarte in Munich, was a notoriously blunt individual and not in any way intimidated by Adolf Hitler.

The rank and file of the SA, he informed his chief, had long been spoiling for a fight and had grumbled to their battalion chiefs that there seemed precious little for them to do.

Brueckner declared: 'The day is coming when I can no longer hold my people. If nothing happens soon they will sneak away.'

They could, Hitler knew, scarcely be blamed. All Germany's assets and resources were being drained to meet the reparations bills. Gold stocks were exhausted; backing for the mark was all but non-existent. The French had snatched the Ruhr and the nation's best earner of foreign currency had gone. On the very day of the Ruhr occupation, the mark stood at 10,400 to the dollar. Three weeks later, the figure had soared to 50,000 and by the end of July, an incredible four million.

For the middle classes it quite literally spelt disaster. The wages paid to the workers were nothing more than waste paper.

And here was Brueckner saying: 'Most of my men are unemployed. They've expended their last garment, their shoes and their last ten pfennigs on training. They look to you to take action to get us out of this mess.'

At first, all Hitler's instincts were against armed intervention. He was no enemy of brute force where it was necessary, but the timing had to be right. Backstairs intrigue, political chicanery – these were the methods whereby the National Socialists would gain power. Violence could be used at the right psychological moment; ill-timed action would ruin all.

But plainly there was little time for delay.

Hitler was by no means the only one to be worried. Gustav Lenk learnt that steel-helmeted Nazi storm-troopers were assembling around Munich. They were being joined eagerly by the more headstrong elements of the Jungsturm Adolf Hitler.

Lenk quickly issued orders that the young members were to stay at home. Those who could be contacted were given tasks that would keep them busy between the various storm-troop centres on the outskirts of the city.

But Lenk pleaded in vain to some of the older youth; if a fight was in prospect they wanted to take part. Enthusiastically, they threw in their lot with the SA who even now were pouring into lorries and trucks for the journey to the beer cellar.

Lenk foresaw disaster and possibly a blood bath. All the months of hard work in building up the Jungsturm would be destroyed in a matter of hours. Even worse, he saw his own career in jeopardy.

At first, though, it looked as if events were playing into Hitler's hands.

Certainly, the importance of the beer hall meeting had not escaped the authorities. A ring of steel had been thrown round the area; a company of police was inside the hall. Seisser suggested its withdrawal, asking: 'What have we got to be afraid of? The presence of police makes it appear that we can't defend ourselves.' After all, he pointed out, everyone from the political centre and right had been invited to the meeting, including both Hitler and that magnificent symbol of the old order of Germany, General Ludendorff.

A compromise was eventually agreed. A troop of forty-five Landespolizei was concealed in a building a quarter of a mile away. A mere patrol took care of the surrounding streets; Hitler's followers were able to report that here was a plum for the picking.

News of the meeting coursed through Bavaria. On the night of 8 November a large crowd, which was considerably greater than Kahr and his aides had expected, jostled to get into the hall. An overspill was inevitable; those unable to gain admittance jostled around in the square in inquisitive, impatient groups.

Inside, all was bustle, general good humour and vast quantities of beer. Waitresses snaked between the tables with armfuls of steins; the air was rich with the ripe fumes of ale and cigar smoke.

Adolf Hitler was there but he did not drink; the stein of beer brought to him by his bodyguard, Ulrich Graf, remained untouched. There were four cronies with Hitler: business manager Max Amman who, along with Josef Gerum and Rudolf Hess, was the veteran of many a street battle, and Ernst (Putzi) Hanfstaengel, a soft-spoken Munich playboy more used to the rarefied atmosphere of a cocktail lounge than an extrovert crowd of beer-swillers.

Hitler was on edge. There were, he felt, far too many people about. The crowd milling around the entrance to the beer cellar would lessen the drama and the impact of a sudden eruption of storm-troopers.

On his way in, Hitler had spotted a police acquaintance; casually, he suggested that it might be wise to keep the square clear in case of trouble.

The policeman conceded it was a sensible precaution and began to shift the crowd. Excellent! There was now a clear path for the SA.

Then all at once Ulrich Graf was at his master's elbow. He had slipped outside to do a swift reconnaissance. He whispered: 'They've arrived!'

The truck crammed with storm-troopers screamed to a halt in the square; men disgorged, catapulting towards the beer hall in one bunched brown mass. The police were puzzled, at first taking the SA for regular Reichswehr forces.

And now other trucks were rumbling into the square. Out tumbled a clutch of Jungsturm recruits, buttressed by the muscle of their SA guardians.

Meanwhile, inside the beer hall, Gustav von Kahr was on the platform, flanked by Lossow and Seisser, together with a knot of their associates.

Hitler and his companions could hear the clatter of the Jungsturm and the SA. The time to act had come.

With a single blow, Hitler sent his stein of beer crashing to the floor. His hand snaked to his pistol holster; he felt the reassuring hard metal of the Browning. His companions did the same. Then Hitler thrust his way to the front of the hall.

It should have been a highly effective piece of theatre. But in fact the crowd was bunched so close that there was barely room to lift elbows from foam-covered tables. In such an atmosphere, Hitler's melodramatic gesture passed virtually unnoticed. Kahr was able to continue with his speech. The entrance of the demon king fell flat as a discarded stein of good Bavarian beer.

Ulrich Graf was the first to seize the initiative. With his formidable bulk, he cleared a path for Hitler, who was by now within sight of the platform.

Kahr stopped in full flood, his voice trailing away. At last, the crowd was aware that something was wrong. A move was made towards the exits; the contingents of the SA and the Jungsturm barred the way.

One of the first to recover was Major Hunglinger, one of Seisser's police aides. He advanced towards Adolf Hitler, his hand travelling swiftly towards his holster.

He never made it. Hitler pressed his own weapon to the other man's forehead, snapping: 'Take your hand out!'

Hunglinger gave way. Hermann Goering, steel helmet crammed on his head, climbed on to a table, kicking the beer out of the way. He bellowed: 'Silence!'

The crowd ignored him. It was Hitler's turn; he lifted his own weapon and sent a single shot crashing into the ceiling. He yelled: 'If silence is not restored, I'll install a machine gun in the gallery.'

The effect was instantaneous; a heavy hush fell on the hall.

What followed next was nothing short of miraculous. Hitler started to speak. It was no mere empty ranting; he set out to woo his audience, initially at least, with sweet reasonableness.

His intention, he claimed, was not directed against Kahr in any way. On the contrary, the man had his full trust and, when the putsch had succeeded, he would be regent of Bavaria.

Then Hitler's voice hardened; a new government must be formed. It would consist of Ludendorff, Lossow, Seisser – and, of course, himself.

An eyewitness in the beer hall, Karl-Alexander von Muller, recounted:

> I cannot remember in my entire life such a change in the attitude of the crowd in a few minutes, almost a few seconds. There were certainly many who were not converted yet. But the sense of the majority had fully reversed itself. Hitler had turned them inside out, with a few sentences. It had almost something of hocus-pocus or magic, about it. Loud approval roared forth, no further opposition was to be heard.

In a daze, Kahr, together with Lossow and Seisser, allowed himself to be shepherded into an ante-room for discussions.

It was to be no gentlemanly, round-the-table parley. Hitler had long ago adopted the role of street fighter and he relished it.

The cowed trio were treated to threats and bullying. Hitler gestured with the Browning: 'There are four rounds left in it – three for the traitors and, if that fails, one for me.'

It was not to be as easy as that. Hitler calmed, cajoled, threatened; the support of the trio was essential. But they remained unmoved – and all the time the crowd waited. Hitler was only too conscious that if it turned impatient and nasty then the day would plainly be lost.

A machine-gun-toting Graf was told to keep the troublesome prisoners under guard. Hitler stalked back into the hall and launched into desperate oratorical wheedling in support of the putsch.

His voice throbbing with emotion, he pleaded: 'Kahr, Lossow and Seisser are struggling hard to reach a decision. May I say to them that you will stand with them?'

The answer was a roaring crescendo: 'Yes! Yes!'

'In a free Germany,' bawled Hitler, 'there is also room for an autonomous Bavaria! I can say this to you. Either the German revolution begins tonight or we will all be dead by dawn.'

Viewed in retrospect, the Beer Hall Putsch had some of the more ridiculous trappings of grand opera; certainly what happened next could hardly have been more theatrical. General Erich Ludendorff, a faintly ludicrous figure resplendent in an Imperial Army uniform heavy with medals, bustled into the beer hall.

The distinguished veteran was faintly resentful at having missed so much of the initial drama. Hitler had need of him; it was essential the old gentleman was soothed and put to work. The General, looking understandably bewildered, was virtually frogmarched into the ante-room to use his persuasive powers on the captured trio.

Whether it was the patriotic fervour of the General or the menacing stance of Ulrich Graf that worked the magic could only be conjectured. The result was that

Kahr, Lossow and Seisser caved in.

They would, they said, cooperate with Adolf Hitler and the Nazis.

Hitler, beside himself with joy, led them all back to the platform. Brief speeches were made and loyalty professed by the released men. Hitler, predictably, was not brief. He yelled that the criminals now in command in Berlin would be destroyed. There would be no rest 'until on the ruins of the wretched Germany of today there should have arisen once more a Germany of power and greatness, of splendour'.

There was much else besides and it was all heady stuff. The crowds were delirious. Those who ran the beer hall had other emotions: mostly relief that business was restored. The orchestra, its members suitably cowed, had stopped playing during the melodrama. Now they eagerly started up again; the beer flowed anew.

Hitler's intoxication was of a different variety: it was emotional and, as it turned out, destructive to his ultimate judgement.

The flush of victory led him to a disastrous blunder.

It was decided as a precaution to take a few hostages just in case anyone had a change of mind during the night. A squad of SA moved in on assorted former ministers, bankers, police chiefs and city councillors.

A suggestion that Kahr, Lossow and Seisser should be included was greeted with horror by Ludendorff.

He protested: 'But these men have given their word as soldiers that they are with us. To doubt them would be an affront to their honour as officers and gentlemen.'

In other circumstances, this was not an argument that would have appealed in the slightest to Adolf Hitler. But nothing could still his mood of euphoria. His guard was down; the three men were allowed to leave the beer hall.

Kahr fled with his aides to the safety of Regensburg, which was proclaimed immediately as the temporary headquarters of the government of Bavaria. Lossow was at the receiving end of the towering fury of Reichswehr Commander-in-Chief General von Seeckt, who ordered: 'If you do not take immediate steps to put down this putsch, I will come down from Berlin and do it for you.'

Elsewhere, the outlook was already black for Hitler. Storm-troopers of one of the fighting leagues, the Bund Oberland, were getting the worst of it from regular troops at the army engineers' barracks.

The victor of the early evening was now becoming more than a little anxious. And with good reason. The dawn that broke over Munich brought little promise to the SA. On to the streets of snow and sleet tramped troop reinforcements from all over Bavaria. Troops and auxiliaries of the SA marching through the grey and muddy streets for a rendezvous at the beer hall were faced with posters denouncing the National Socialists as a proscribed party.

Kahr had wasted little time. An emergency edition of the Munich *Post*, condemning any association with General Ludendorff and Adolf Hitler, was rushed on to the streets.

In the beer hall itself, the spirits of Hitler, Ludendorff and Goering plunged. A meeting which had been arranged with Lossow at the beer hall at midnight had not been kept. What had happened?

They were soon to find out. A radio message from army headquarters to Berlin was intercepted. The putschists not only learnt that the three former prisoners had double-crossed them; warrants were also out for the arrest of Hitler, Ludendorff and others involved.

Elsewhere came news of Reichswehr reinforcements arriving at the stations. What was the use of the rhetoric and bluster of the SA and Jungsturm bully-boys now? They were revealed for what they were: a bunch of aggressive louts who would be crushed by field guns and armoured cars, to say nothing of disciplined regular troops.

Hitler was for putting out renewed feelers to Kahr and Lossow; mediation until the next chance presented itself.

Ludendorff shook his head. He was for the grand gesture. He said: 'We will march on the city.'

The suggestion evoked protest. An attempt to do anything so foolish would surely only lead to violence. Armed troops would open fire.

Ludendorff, the German hero who had led his people to great victories on both the eastern and western fronts, bridled with indignation. He proclaimed: 'The heavens will fall before the Bavarian Reichswehr turns against me.'

Hitler shrugged: 'What else can we do? There has been no word from Lossow. We march.'

And they did. It was towards 11 o'clock on the morning of 9 November, the anniversary of the proclamation of the German Republic, that Hitler, Ludendorff and Goering led a three-thousand-strong column of storm-troopers out of the gardens of the beer hall and headed towards the centre of Munich.

At the head of the column was proudly unfurled a Swastika flag and a banner of the Bund Oberland. The storm-troopers carried carbines, some slung over their shoulders, some with fixed bayonets.

The atmosphere of black farce persisted; there was something decidedly ludicrous about the unimpressive figure of the future Fuehrer of the Third Reich whose sole armament was a brandished revolver.

Ludendorff strolled out with confident arrogance, for all the world as if he was still commanding some of Germany's finest troops. He stared with disdain at the line of police blocking the progress of the march.

Now the man of the moment was Hermann Goering.

He snapped at the head of the police contingent: 'We have a number of hostages in the rear. One shot from you and we'll kill the lot.'

The police commander knew about the hostages that had been scooped up by the Nazis. He had no way, though, of knowing whether they were actually in the procession. Either way, the police broke ranks; the march carried on.

The objective was the war ministry. Ernst Roehm and some of his men were pinned down there by the Reichswehr; both sides were armed and both sides consisted of old soldiers who knew one another. Nobody had the stomach to open fire.

The ministry turned out to be no easy target. Furthermore, at this point Hitler and his followers were at a serious disadvantage. They had to pass through the Residentstrasse, an extremely narrow thoroughfare. It was the obvious place to station a fresh contingent of the crack Green Police in the charge of Freiherr von Godin.

Nevertheless, the Nazis made an effort to talk their way through. Ulrich Graf stepped forward, shouting urgently: 'Don't shoot! His Excellency Ludendorff is coming!'

But the magic of a famous name this time failed to work. Godin was a policeman, not a soldier. He snapped: 'What do my men carry a rifle for? I do what I'm paid to.'

He rapped out an order. First came the single shot. Then there was the volley with a bullet crashing into the skull of Max Erwin von Scheubner-Richter, one of Hitler's closest cronies. Goering crashed to the pavement with a serious thigh wound. A fresh volley tore into the storm-troopers, killing a member of the Jungsturm Adolf Hitler. The organisation which was to become the Hitler Youth had claimed its first martyr.

Hitler, nursing a dislocated shoulder, was bundled

33

hastily into a car which had been shadowing the procession. It streaked away; left on the pavement were sixteen of his followers.

But within a few days all the rebel leaders had been rounded up. Hitler was sent for trial. His National Socialist Party dissolved, the leader, who had to share responsibility for the bungling of the enterprise, languished in Landsberg jail, high above the River Lech.

In the absence of his chief, Gustav Lenk tried desperately to keep the youth movement in Bavaria together. There could of course be no question of the Jungsturm Adolf Hitler continuing under that name. Lenk tried to launch it under the banner of the Patriotic Youth Association of Greater Germany, but this merely had the unhappy effect of drawing police attention to him.

The authorities swooped. Lenk was arrested; he too ended up in Landsberg, but was released a month later. His chief was paroled at the same time.

Things could never be quite the same again between them. Hitler took to his heart some sympathetic remarks made at his trial by the state prosecutor, Dr Steinglen: 'It is understandable that enthusiastic youth suffers from impatience. But youth must be disciplined and led in the right direction by mature men. Impatience must be replaced by the ability to work quietly and confidently for the future, waiting with clenched teeth until the hour is ripe.'

Hitler waited two months before stepping back into the Bavarian public limelight as leader of the National Socialist Party, whose banning had been removed on promise of good behaviour. Back in Landsberg, he had written in his political testimony *Mein Kampf*: 'I had decided to rebuild the youth movement as an integral part of the National Socialist Party.'

The dream of a new fully integrated 'Hitler Youth' was one step nearer reality.

6

The gates of Landsberg jail had barely slammed shut behind Adolf Hitler after his sentence before a fierce power struggle within the by now seriously disorganised Nazi youth movement threatened to tear it asunder completely.

The writing was on the wall for Gustav Lenk; his enthusiasm for a Jungsturm role in the Beer Hall Putsch, soon to be glorified in Nazi mythology, had been less than total. He had been heard to say of the man who was now known as 'Fuehrer': 'Hitler's position as leader of the National Socialists is not sufficiently strong to survive. Youth cannot depend on him.'

This amounted to nothing less than treason. But the murder of political opponents, which was to become commonplace after Hitler secured the office of Chancellor, was not yet practical. Lenk would have to be removed by other means.

The overweaning personal ambition of the one-time piano-polisher proved his undoing. He made moves to set up his own political group, founding the so-called German Defence Organisation, independent of the NSDAP.

A whispering campaign was launched, centring on alleged misappropriation of party funds. It proved enough; Lenk was pushed out of the youth movement altogether.

In desperation, he begged the party newspaper to print a news item in which he announced his own resignation. The request was refused; Lenk's active role was at an end.

All of which was mightily approved by another ambitious young man on the make, a twenty-one-year-old law student named Kurt Gruber, who had taken no part in the Munich putsch and had built up the Greater German Youth Movement in Plauen, part of an area known as 'Red Saxony' with a history of strong Communist revolutionary agitation. But Gruber's allegiance was staunch to Hitler as his unquestioned leader.

In Saxony alone his largely working-class movement consisted of around 2,500; he had even held his own rally in Plauen. And his youthful adherents had their own uniform, which included the brown shirt and a Swastika-emblazoned armlet of a design distinct from that of the storm-troopers.

Hitler may not have liked the existence of the Greater German Youth Movement but he could scarcely afford to ignore its strength; beyond Thuringia and Saxony, there were branches in Franconia, the Rhineland and the Palatinate. What was more, Gruber had the all-important financial backing. Money was poured generously into his coffers in Saxony by a local textile manufacturer, Martin Mutschmann, who had been a National Socialist since 1923 and was destined to become a Gauleiter.

In spite of himself, Hitler found it all very impressive. During July 1926, he told assembled party formations of the importance of the task of winning over German youth. But it was to be youth kept in check. The Sturmabteilung still lurked, the baleful brown legions of storm-troopers whose muscle-power and dedication to uncomplicated brutality had already proved useful in many a fist-fight on the Munich streets.

The SA was the power and the engine of National Socialism – to it, Hitler reasoned, ultimately belonged the task of moulding the young legions. A distinctive

36

Swastika armband might be permitted; independence must go no further.

Plainly, the awesomely ambitious and energetic Gruber needed someone to keep him in check. Hitler's choice fell on a Freikorps veteran from Westphalia, Hauptmann Franz Felix Pfeffer von Salomon, first Gauleiter of the Ruhr.

Hitler's instructions to Salomon were concise. He told him: 'Forget all those ambitions about modelling the SA on the army. It must become a party and political formation. And that applies to the youth group. The ultimate purpose is to make National Socialism a mass movement.'

The Fuehrer went on to marshal his lieutenants to do just that. Events moved even faster than the wily Gruber had expected. Prompted by a suggestion of the notorious Jew-baiter and Franconian Gauleiter Julius Streicher, Gruber's youth organisation was renamed Hitler-Jugend, Bund der Deutschen Arbeiterjugend.

The Hitler Youth proper was born.

What was more, it was a birth at high speed. From regional head of the youth movement of the NSDAP, Kurt Gruber was not so much promoted as propelled to the job of Reichsfuehrer of the Hitler Youth and adviser on all matters relating to youth in Munich.

It was an extraordinary promotion for a young man of twenty-three and Gruber might well have been forgiven if he had allowed it even temporarily to go to his head.

But the new Reichsfuehrer of the Hitler Youth was a shrewd political tactician. He could have established himself in Munich; instead he elected to keep his headquarters at Plauen. After all, he reasoned, in the shifting sands of Bavarian politics you never knew when a swift exit or change of allegiance might be necessary.

The Hitler Youth Reich Command at Plauen was responsible not just for Saxony but for the whole of Germany and Austria. It soon got busy. Fourteen separate departments sprang into being; there was one for education, welfare, military and sport. Hitler Youth groups for those under fourteen years of age also had their own department, as did female members, whose interests were looked after by two girls.

Gruber undertook a gruelling travel itinerary throughout Germany and in Czechoslovakia and Poland, cementing contacts within the youth movements established by his predecessor.

Yet he did have a nagging worry that could not be banished easily by ceaseless activity. Salomon was equally tireless and losing no time in fulfilling his brief from Hitler to subordinate the Hitler Youth to the SA.

There was, Gruber felt sure, bound to be a clash sooner or later. He decided to meet it head on. A summit meeting of leaders of Hitler Youth was called at Weimar in December 1926. Gruber made sure Salomon was invited. The tact and charm of his SA superior utterly disarmed Gruber. Of course, said Salomon smoothly, the Hitler Youth and SA were brothers: naturally the hand of fraternal friendship was extended. By the end of the day, Salomon had a ready collaborator.

Once he was certain that Gruber would eat out of his hand, Salomon pleasantly put forward some 'propositions'. Any Hitler Youth member above the age of eighteen would, he explained, be required to join the NSDAP as well. What was more, all promotions to the higher ranks of the Hitler Youth would require party agreement.

Gruber, of course, recognised it as a further clipping of his wings. On the other hand, to be tucked securely under the party umbrella was no bad thing. The thugs of the Sturmabteilung who kicked and bullied opponents in dark alleys could be bad enemies.

As if to banish Gruber's misgivings, Hitler went out of

his way to emphasise his admiration for his youth movement.

The party rally held in Nuremberg between 19 and 21 August 1927 was a high spot in the history of Nazism and above all in the chequered saga of the Hitler Youth.

Three hundred of their ranks paraded before Adolf Hitler at the rally. Their Fuehrer paid fulsome tribute to the patriotism and unselfishness of his young followers, many of whom had made the long journey to the event on foot, while other echelons of the party had made use of special trains.

To an outsider, it would have seemed that fresh young faces were not much in evidence; after all, the Hitler Youth represented only one per cent of the thirty thousand storm-troopers there that day.

But Kurt Gruber was well pleased. Hitler Youth was at last beginning to stand on its own as a movement with a distinctive character.

Later, he was to write in the publication *National-sozialistische Monatshefte*:

At this time organisation as an end in itself ceased. The idea began to be effective. Young men worked and managed to give the Hitler Youth a face of its own. Soon one could see the results and successes of this untiring tough work; signs of its own life became evident in the Hitler Youth. The continuous participation with the SA and the party ceased. The boys started 'to go on their own hikes', to hold their own meetings and gatherings – in their own fashion.

It all seemed very impressive. But most of Bavaria, let alone the rest of Germany, viewed the Hitler Youth with a tolerant smile; surely it was a bit much to expect anybody to take these glorified boy scouts over-seriously. Neither at this time did it look as if National Socialism would amount to much, either. Revolution seemed arid and pointless; the Weimar Republic, after all, was on a prosperous run. There was a splurge of new airfields, new theatres, new sports stadiums and swimming pools. It was on borrowed money, but nobody cared. The Republic could plainly afford it.

Doubters were told to look at the figures. Output, which in 1923 had dropped to 55 per cent of that in 1913, climbed to 122 per cent by 1927. Unemployment plunged to under a million in 1928. Retail sales were up 25 per cent over 1925. And why not?

No one seemed to care now about those disgruntled, lower-middle-class misfits who had huddled into the meeting halls of the German Workers' Party less than a decade ago. They had been among the millions of shop-keepers and low-wage earners whom Hitler had been keen to draw on for mass support. Nobody, it was argued, wanted his brand of ranting nationalism now.

The May elections of 1928 had underlined the point; the result for the NSDAP was a bare twelve seats in the Reichstag.

The main consolation – and it was considerable – was that in four years Hitler's movement had mushroomed from 27,000 to 108,000 members, and what was especially welcome to the NSDAP was that it had not been confined to Bavaria but had reached out to all parts of Germany.

Although the immediate political outlook was less than bright, Adolf Hitler was more than content to bide his time. The tide, he felt confident, would turn.

Kurt Gruber, rapidly becoming stupefied with his administrative responsibilities and gruelling travel schedules, was less sanguine. But for different reasons. For Gruber in his turn had come up against a potentially dangerous rival.

*

At first sight, there had seemed nothing remotely threatening about Baldur von Schirach. The pleasant open face with its ice-cream smoothness suggested frankness itself. The celebrated American journalist and pre-war Berlin correspondent William Shirer wrote: 'Baldur von Schirach . . . looked rather like a sleek, shallow American college boy, the kind who made a good cheer leader at football games.' He had the self-satisfied look of someone who has never known the sharpest edge of poverty. The dirt of the sidewalks, scene of so many punch-ups between rival youth movements in Weimar Germany, never stained the crisp executive suit which would not have been out of place on Madison Avenue.

There was in fact American ancestry: his mother's side included two signatories to the Declaration of Independence and a grandfather who had been a Union officer casualty at the Battle of Bull Run.

The military lines went back further. Baldur's father, Carl Bailey-Norris von Schirach, had been an officer in the Garde-Kuerassier Regiment of Wilhelm II. It was not a life, however, that would ever have appealed to someone of Baldur's rather naive romanticism – mirrored in membership of the Young Germans League, which claimed spiritual sympathy with the Wandervoegel and was much given to energetic hikes and sentimental campfire singsongs.

But the concept of simple comradeship and idealistic patriotism withered under the disillusion brought by the war. Afterwards, there was bitter railing against the iniquities of the Treaty of Versailles and the misdeeds of the Communists and the Jews. In Munich he heard speakers voicing the same sort of sentiments – there was Nazism's eventual resident philosopher, the Balt Alfred Rosenberg, and that same Streicher who had suggested the name of Hitler Youth.

With uncritical eagerness, the plump and pliable Schirach waded into the mass of anti-Semitic literature –

Henry Ford's *The International Jew*, Houston S. Chamberlain's *The Foundations of the Nineteenth Century* and, it need hardly be said, Adolf Hitler's *Mein Kampf*.

The Fuehrer's book had Schirach hooked. From then on he accepted Hitler and his aims root and branch.

Such unquestioning subservience was worth exploiting and Hitler on their first meeting in 1926 did not hesitate to do so. He advised the young man earnestly: 'Go to Munich. There is the beating heart of our movement.'

Schirach's eyes were on Munich's University, where he intended to read German and the history of art. Apart from his studies, there would be a chance to use the university as a recruiting ground for the ranks of the SA, which he had joined at eighteen.

The engaging schoolboy grin and puppy-like charm scarcely endeared him to the street-fighting echelons of the storm-troopers. The dislike was mutual and Schirach did not find a warm haven in the National Socialist Student Association, either. His credentials were hardly promising: he had never earned his own living and was considered totally out of touch with the working classes.

It did not bother him. He was already looking two steps ahead. He wanted the leadership of the Student Association and, through it, a far greater prize – Hitler Youth itself.

In the meantime, there was still the little matter of Kurt Gruber.

It was in the pride of a brilliant summer's day that two thousand of the Hitler Youth filed past their Fuehrer for the 1929 party rally. Admittedly, half of them were from Austria, but there were also strong delegations from Saxony and Berlin Brandenburg. Of great significance was the achievement of the contingent from the German capital; in what was to become the annual ritual of the

Adolf-Hitler Marsch, the Hitler Youth covered the entire four-hundred-mile journey from Berlin to Nuremberg on foot.

Proudly handed over were new Hitler Youth banners depicting an eagle holding a black crossed hammer and sword on a red background.

Everywhere at the rally, Schirach was active, developing his innate propensity for intrigue.

The previous July, he had succeeded in ousting Wilhelm Tempel as Reichsfuehrer of the National Socialist Student Association. The first of his goals had been achieved; he now went ahead to secure the other.

Behind the backs of Hitler and Gruber, Schirach had sent out circular letters to other nationalist groups bidding for members.

When news of this leaked out, Gruber retaliated by visiting as many leaders as he could, speaking during March and April 1929 at thirty-two Hitler Youth rallies throughout Germany.

As for Schirach, at the party rally he and his mentor Rosenberg invited leaders of youth leagues to a key meeting in Nuremberg.

At the meeting, Schirach was told coldly: 'We regard your group not as socialist or revolutionary, but organised along élitist lines.

'We would not fuse with *you*, but would expect you to fuse with us. Fusion must mean submergence with the Hitler Youth, nothing less.'

Gruber believed that he had beaten off any opposition. He could argue with some justification that his achievements were formidable. He was able to point out to Hitler that from eighty branches in 1926, he had expanded the Hitler Youth by 1929 to approximately 450 branches, and membership had risen from 700 in 1926 to 13,000 in 1929.

He had won a concession from Pfeffer von Salomon that eighteen-year-old Hitler Youth members were no longer obliged to transfer to the SA. It meant an even greater degree of independence.

Two events were to stand Gruber's world on its head: the return to the SA of Hauptmann Ernst Roehm and the eclipse of Pfeffer von Salomon.

Ernst Roehm looked out on the world from a pair of small, alert eyes, deep set within a huge double-chinned round face, flushed and blood-flecked. But what grabbed the attention was the deep scar slashing in a broad cleft from the left cheek-bone. A short, stiff, triangular moustache concealed an extra long upper lip which shadowed a broad tight mouth.

Roehm strode through life with a sort of dissolute bravado. His homosexuality was flagrant; he surrounded himself with youths chosen for their considerable physical beauty. If they were not wholly corrupted by the time they joined Roehm's entourage he lost no time in completing the process.

News of his predilections had found its way into the anti-Nazi press, which gleefully paraded them by publishing love letters to one of his boys.

Hitler was keen to build up the SA into an at least superficially 'respectable' movement as a preliminary to gaining power. This sort of publicity did his case no good at all; indignantly, the Fuehrer questioned his old comrade, who had joined the party in the very earliest days and was widely regarded as a close crony.

Roehm did not resent Hitler's questions. He merely leered: 'Adolf, you can certainly say that I'm bisexual.' Hitler dropped the matter. After all, at this time no one could afford undue moral scruples. Besides, Adolf Hitler had need of Ernst Roehm.

In 1925, there had been a rift. Roehm had gone off to join the Bolivian army as a lieutenant-colonel. Five years later, Hitler had begged him to return and take over the leadership of the SA. Salomon had turned out to lack the vital ruthlessness; far too many of the storm-troopers, including their leaders, believed that a coming Nazi revolution could only be achieved through force. Hitler was playing a waiting game, exploiting the political weaknesses of opponents. Increasingly, the SA had taken to the streets to molest and murder. It helped the cause not at all.

They needed a firm hand. The fact that the SA had to be administered by a sexual pervert whose gluttony at banquets attended by fawning catamites was of course regrettable, but Roehm's seemingly inflexible loyalty and lack of scruples were indispensable.

A year after his recall, it certainly seemed that Roehm was more than earning his keep. By then he had created thirty-four Gausturm units and ten SA-Gruppen, which placed under his orders a formidable force of four hundred thousand men.

In return, Roehm made it clear that he wanted closer control over the Hitler Youth. There must be none of this nonsensical talk about independence. That was possible in the early days when the National Socialists were struggling for recognition as a political party, but tight discipline was necessary now.

Baldur von Schirach saw a golden opportunity to discredit Kurt Gruber. He sided openly with Roehm; a slander campaign aganst Gruber was launched.

It proved effective. Hitler struck without warning.

A peremptory directive was issued on 27 April 1931. From now on Gruber would be directly subordinate to Roehm as Chief of Staff of the SA. What was more, Roehm had to approve the appointment of senior members of the Hitler Youth.

And for Gruber there was a fresh blow. The retention of the Hitler Youth headquarters away from Munich could no longer be tolerated. Such independence as Gruber had so far managed to preserve was at an end.

For Gruber, whose hot temper was notorious, it was

the last straw. He confronted Roehm.

The leader of the SA snapped: 'You can command at the very most 25,000 followers. The figures for the NSDAP speak for themselves.'

It was true, and not just among rank-and-file party members. New elections in Germany in September 1930 had been held in the shadow of the world economic recession. Although the Social Democrats had remained the largest single party, the NSDAP had taken second place with 107 seats in the Reichstag. The tide was turning for the Nazis.

Gruber's response sealed his own fate. Rashly, he promised to double Hitler Youth membership to 50,000 by the end of 1931. It was an impossible undertaking. The news from headquarters in Munich of Gruber's 'resignation' was not long in coming.

Gruber, not even aware that his job was in question, read of his own departure in the morning papers.

It was the outcome of a squalid power battle. Hitler was anxious to divert attention from it and published a swift new directive:

Within the framework of the Supreme SA Command a new office Reichsjugendfuehrer has been created. The Reichsjugendfuehrer is directly responsible to the Chief of Staff of the SA. To the post of Reichs-jugendfuehrer I appoint party member Schirach . . . He keeps the Chief of Staff informed about all organisational problems of the youth formations with special emphasis on those affairs which involve the SA. His rank is that of a Gruppenfuehrer, his uniform has yet to be determined.

Schirach now also had under his umbrella the National Socialist Student Association and the National Socialist Pupils Association.

It was an impressive power base. It seemed at last as if

the Hitler Youth refrain 'Tomorrow belongs to us' could become decidedly more than a romantic dream. The cost though was increasingly to be spelt out in blood and violence.

7

The dawn had broken cold and unappealing above the mean streets of Berlin's Wedding district.

But the bleak Sunday of 26 January 1932 did not blunt a day of pride and high adventure for Herbert Norkus of the Hitler Youth, thrilled to be serving alongside his taxi-driver father, who was already in the SA. Herbert and his friends had been given a definite job. That week there was to be a key party meeting at which prominent Hitler Youth leaders would speak on such weighty subjects as 'Swastika or Soviet Star' and 'What we want'.

Herbert was detailed with his troop to billpost the streets advertising the meeting. So absorbed was the group that scant notice was taken of the motorcycle which passed them, returned and then sped off.

The appraising glance of the rider might have served as a warning. But it was already too late.

Wedding – 'Red Wedding' as it had long been known – was a notorious Communist enclave with its own youth contingents. Now they were on the streets and there was barely time to scatter before the knives were out and flashing.

Herbert was not fast enough. Someone grabbed him by the hair, dragged him into an alley and beat him soundly. Then as he tried to crawl away, the repeated stabbings began. However, across the road there was a house. Herbert groped towards it, leaving a fresh trail of blood and hand prints across the wall.

The door was opened in response to his frightened knocks; the scared householder promptly slammed it shut. There was nothing for Herbert Norkus to do now but crawl away and die. But even that was denied him. The killers came back, dragging him off for another orgy of stabbing and mutilation.

The autopsy at the Moabit hospital revealed five stab wounds in the back, two in the chest. The face of the dead youth was a bloody pulp with the upper lip wrenched away.

Herbert Norkus was just twelve years old.

To many, it had been seemingly innocent boy scout fun to attend camps and parades and bonfires and then at the end of the day to stand and sing the stirring 'Fahrenlieder' – marching songs – which Schirach himself had written:

> We march for Hitler through night and suffering
> With the banner of freedom and bread,
> Our banner means more to us than death.

In the final, dying months of the Weimar Republic, the words were transformed into grim reality.

The statistics spelt it out: when the Red Front and the storm-troopers faced one another in the district of Prussia between 1 June and 20 July 1932, there were 322 acts of terror, leading to 72 deaths and 497 serious injuries.

The Reichsbanner Black, Red and Gold, the para-military organisation of the Social Democrats, was also involved in the clashes.

The violence coursed far beyond Berlin and Munich. In Kiel, Hitler Youth members who were butchers' apprentices donned their bloodstained white aprons to do battle with the Red Front. From the headquarters of Hitler Youth came the call to the streets: 'With your banners flying, come to us, the youth of the German workers, fight with us against the old system, against the old world order, against the old generation.

'Fight for us, for Socialism, for freedom and for bread!'

While young bones continued to be broken on the city pavements, Adolf Hitler was manoeuvring towards ultimate power. Shortly before noon on 30 January 1933, he drove to the Chancellery for an interview with President Paul von Hindenburg. Hitler had forged a successful alliance with the Nationalists and the forces of the German Right. At noon precisely, the President, acting properly within the constitution, entrusted the Chancellorship to Adolf Hitler.

To anyone who served in the Hitler Youth, no matter what happened later, memories of that evening were indelible.

This indeed was Germany's moment of triumph. The aggressively confident sons now marched in shirts of khaki, whereas their infinitely gentler fathers had donned Bavarian costumes as members of the Wander-voegel. But that was a world away; now Hitler's programme of corruption could bite deep and unchecked.

And with their comrades in the SA, the delirious Hitler Youth marched that evening from dusk until long past midnight. A torchlight parade of tens of thousands snaked from the depths of the Tiergarten, under the triumphal arch of the Brandenburg Gate and down the entire length of the Wilhelmstrasse.

And there were the songs – the 'Horst Wessel' and the other Fahrenlieder – together with the banners and the crash and the thud of jackboots beating out their harsh rhythm on the pavements.

The light of the torches illuminated the fresh young faces of a generation to whom Hitler cried out: 'We must be dominated by one will, we must form one unity, we must be held together by one discipline; we must all be filled with one obedience; one subordination.'

And the same lights also lit up the enraptured onlookers who crammed the streets. Hitler had been embraced by them all willingly and joyfully and there were few who would have contradicted Joseph Goebbels, scribbling in his diary at the next day's dawn: 'It is almost a dream . . . a fairy tale . . . The new Reich has been born. Fourteen years of work have been crammed with victory.

'The German revolution has begun.'

Hitler had been in power barely five months when he gave Schirach the new and more grandiose title of Jugendfuehrer des Deutschen Reiches – Youth Leader of Germany.

The title was no mere ornament. His office had the task of supervising the entire youth activities of a Germany daily becoming Nazified. No new youth organisation could be formed without Schirach's permission; needless to say, he never gave it. The official policy was 'Gleichstellung' – a term which could be politely interpreted as the gradual 'coordination' and 'integration' of all other youth organisations into the Hitler Youth, together with a total ban on any organisations outside it.

Gleichstellung could often lead to acts verging on thuggery.

Young Karl Nabersberg, swelling with pride under the twin authority of a khaki uniform and the recently created rank of Gebietsfuehrer – district leader – might well have been forgiven for believing that his hour of destiny had arrived. Jugendfuehrer Schirach had actually entrusted to him the key task of occupying the offices of the Reichs Committee of the German Youth Associations in Berlin's Alsenstrasse.

This organisation would prove a rich prize; it was said to have a membership of over six million boys and girls. So far it obstinately refused to have anything to do with Gleichstellung; it was about to be taught a lesson.

Nabersberg swiftly mustered fifty suitably aggressive members of Hitler Youth, instructing them to barge into the committee's offices.

The result began with near farce. No reconnaissance had been attempted: neither Hermann Maas, the business manager, nor any of his assistants were at work that day.

The nonplussed youths were faced with equally puzzled office staff, many old enough to be their parents. One particularly unhappy boy, put in charge by Nabersberg, politely asked a clerk whether he could use the waste-paper basket for his sandwich papers.

Meanwhile, Nabersberg had located Maas elsewhere in Berlin; the wretched secretary was abruptly ordered back to his office.

Protests were drowned in a volley of abuse. Then came the order to Maas: 'Pack up your things and don't ever come back.'

Maas accepted without a word; the by now suitably cowed staff were ordered to get on with their work.

For Schirach the entire operation had been well worth it, not so much because six million young people had been absorbed at a stroke into Hitler Youth, but because the files of the committee yielded valuable material on opponents.

Other organisations received similar treatment, even the politically uncommitted ones. Prominent among these was the Greater German Youth League, led by Admiral von Trotha, a veteran of the Kaiser's navy.

Schirach recorded with intolerable smugness: 'This admirable and meritorious man adapted himself to the new situation by virtue of his soldierly sense of duty and his love for the younger generation.'

Just what would be in store for opponents was spelt out by Schirach in an order of 5 July 1933:

I hereby forbid any interference of the Hitler Youth with other youth associations. If the behaviour of members of other youth associations gives cause for complaint then the complaint is to be directed to me through the proper official channels. Insofar as complaints necessitate further action I shall initiate the necessary steps through the appropriate state institutions.

It was not long before any move to spurn the overture of the Hitler Youth became positively dangerous. Members of dissenting organisations in Wiesbaden received from Schirach the following summons:

The Hitler Youth comes to you today with the question: why are you still outside its ranks? We take it that you accept our Fuehrer, Adolf Hitler. But you can only do this if you also accept the Hitler Youth created by him. If you are not willing to join the Hitler Youth then write to us on the enclosed blank.

It would have been most unwise to have done any such thing. For the blank was a form calling for the signature of the father and son and a statement of where both were working. The form would barely have been returned before there was a visit from the Gestapo and the risk of removal to a concentration camp.

Dissent in Nazi Germany was on a level with high treason.

That certain softness in Baldur von Schirach was a quality he soon learned to turn to advantage; it disarmed unwary opponents with deadly effectiveness. His flair for organisation was accompanied by a streak of brutality shared by anyone with a successful career in the

jungle world of the brownshirts. He was only too conscious that Hitler had expressed some impatience at the
comparatively slow growth of the Nazi youth movement
up to 1932, the last year of the Weimar Republic, when it
numbered around 100,000. This had been a puny
statistic compared to the ten *million* enrolled in various
other organisations.

Schirach knew this would have to change if he was to
survive. From now on everything, including time spent
with his family, had to be subordinated to the moulding
of National Socialist youth.

Henriette von Schirach, Baldur's wife, wrote after the
war in her memoirs:

> As far as I was concerned, the Hitler Youth was a
> crowd of boys and girls who had turned up wherever
> Baldur showed himself – singing, asking for auto-
> graphs or hoping to be photographed with him . . . I
> had always felt that I had to share Baldur's affection
> with the Hitler Youth.

The Nazification of the German child began even
before he was eligible to join the Deutsches Jungvolk,
preparatory to entering the Hitler Youth proper at
fourteen. Before that he was a 'Pimpf' (Austrian term
for 'shrimp') but that by no means meant that his education and treatment approximated to the benevolent
junior or preparatory school in other countries.

A Pimpf's initiation test, after which he received his
first ceremonial dagger, consisted of learning and
reciting key passages of Nazi dogma, together with
verses from the 'Horst Wessel Lied'. It was not long
before an infant head was also having to take in the rules
of elementary war games, endless reading – and, above
all, fund-raising, which meant taking part in collection
drives for waste paper and scrap metal.

A favourite story was soon circulating among the

parents of Pimpfs about the mother of a ten-year-old who had asked her son to play with the little girl next door, only to be given the answer: 'It's out of the question. I'm in uniform.'

By the end of 1933, in addition to the youth organisations affiliated to political parties, which were speedily proscribed by the fledgling Third Reich, twenty previously independent youth leagues had widely dissolved and transferred their members into the Hitler Youth. Schirach, now firmly established as Jugendfuehrer, was head of the Reichsjugendfuehrung, a vast bureaucratic body controlling a series of territorial commands, the Obergebiet and Gebiet. Originally, these commands conformed to the composition of the eighteen states of the German Reich, of which the largest was Prussia, occupying more than half of Germany's total area.

To accommodate the more densely populated regions, some of the territorial commands had been subdivided into more simplified zones. The Gebiet of Saxony, for instance, was structured into five Obergebiets, which were the main controlling commands of the area.

A Hitler Youth member would identify his Gebiet area with a cloth triangle badge on his left shoulder sleeve. The Gebiet proper was on a lower line; the actual operational command and the Obergebiet on the upper line.

A chain of command was observed with maximum seriousness; at the head of each was a Gebietsfuehrer, who was also Jungvolk Gebietsfuehrer, since his command extended to the juniors.

Then came the unit strengths within the Hitler Youth and the Jungvolk, dominated by Kameradschaft, usually consisting of some fifteen boys. There were also units designated Schar, Gefolgschaft, Unterbann and Bann, each in the care of an individual Fuehrer.

Girls from ten to fourteen enrolled as Jungmaedel – Young Maidens – and their training included long marches with heavy packs and solid indoctrination in every aspect of Nazi ideology. At fourteen, they were available for the Bund Deutscher Maedchen, the senior branch.

Hitler had urged Schirach: 'Girls must be told of their coming role as women in the Third Reich. Above all, they must become healthy mothers of healthy Nordic children.'

Enforced takeovers of other German youth organisations had, of course, helped a good deal with the recruitment problem.

But Schirach remained uneasy. He had succeeded in the not inconsiderable task of manoeuvring the Hitler Youth away from the overtures of Ernst Roehm and his brownshirts. He considered his own power reasonably assured, but there were anxieties. There was still considerable opposition to the Nazified youth movement, not only from parents who believed their children were being subtly converted into para-military thugs, but from church leaders who complained that the sheer volume of Hitler Youth activities, particularly at weekends, was helping to thin out congregations.

There was a call for a vast campaign of recruitment – and fast.

Schirach seized on 20 April 1936 as a target date to present his master with the most spectacular birthday present the Fuehrer had ever received – every single boy and girl in the Reich who had been born in 1926. All would be invited to 'volunteer' to join the Jungvolk and the Jungmaedel.

The culmination of the campaign was a forceful demonstration of Schirach's flair for organisation and stage management. As a magnificent and sombre backdrop for the official celebration, the Jugendfuehrer chose the Ordensburg in Marienburg, in East Prussia, near the Polish frontier. It was an appropriate choice – the Ordensburgen were the so-called order castles of the Third Reich.

To enter them was to be trapped in a bizarre time machine which hastened the visitor back down the centuries, back to the Order of the Teutonic Knights of the fourteenth and fifteenth centuries. The knightly order was based on the principle of total obedience to the Ordenmeister, who decreed German conquest of the Slavic lands which lay in the east and the enslavement of its peoples.

It was an intimidating site, ripe for malign adaptation by the architects of Nazism and the ideal of Aryan purity. Normally, only the élite of the élite were allowed here, the most fanatical National Socialists of all, who would be taught that the ultimate glorious destiny of Germany lay in those dark Slav lands.

But now more recruits were to be vouchsafed a glimpse of the Ordensburg. Amid sombre light from candles and torches, the new members of the Jungvolk stood in awe, swearing the oath they were to repeat each 20 April, including 1945:

I promise
In the Hitler Youth
To do my duty
At all times
In love and faithfulness
To help the Fuehrer
So help me God.

The oath taken was orchestrated by fifes, drum and fanfares and the refrain *'Vorwaerts, vorwaerts, schmettern die hellen Fanfaren'* – 'Forward, forward, call the fanfares'.

The programme mapped out for the young recruits over the following weeks and months appalled parents who had fondly believed that, aside from the camps and the parades and the ideological harangues, the Hitler Youth was merely a sophisticated boy scout movement.

On the rare occasions members went home, they proudly brandished knives shaped like Wehrmacht daggers and uniforms with Jungvolk insignia and the inevitable brown shirt.

Dedication to the Jungsturm became total. Adults soon had good cause to fear those children who seemed to be growing up so fast and looking at the grown-up world with arrogance and contempt. Respect which their elders had taken for granted began to melt away.

A striking example was provided by a booklet, *Deutsches Volk*, published in Halle. It featured a page photograph of Reichsjugendfuehrer Schirach, below which was printed: 'The meaning of our lives let us proclaim: The war preserved us for the coming war.'

But it was not this that was calculated to freeze the blood. The booklet recounted the story of Karl, a Jungsturm member, who decided, because it was raining, that he would not attend National Youth Day but would go to school instead.

A Jungvolk member took up the story:

Quick march to Karl's house. 'Karl!' we all shout in chorus. Karl is apparently asleep and has not heard us. The hollow drums boom, the bugles blast out a fanfare, and through it all the boys go on shouting for Karl. Now an anxious figure is sighted behind the curtain – Karl's mother – 'Lord, what will the neighbours say? Karl's not here, he's at school, where he ought to be!'

'No, today he ought to be with us.'

A moment of reflection, and we have a plan. We march on singing, and halt outside the school.

'Keep your ranks.'

The leader mounts the steps. His heavy footsteps

can be heard right out in the street. Now they are silent. A knock can be heard.

The leader goes up to the teacher and demands that Karl shall be handed over. The head teacher is horrified, but what can he do but let Karl go? A door bangs to. Now the leader appears on the street with Karl. The two of them stand facing the motionless troop. Dead silence, and then the leader speaks.

'Your place is with the German Jungvolk. We must steel ourselves. And you stay away just because of a few drops of rain! We take our duty very seriously . . . We are not a children's creche. You have shown today, Karl, that you're not yet fit to be one of us. You are suspended until further notice.

'Right wheel! Quick march!'

The marching steps . . . thunder down the street.

The incident might have raised a smile from some adult bystanders; but in fact it was no laughing matter. Karl had directly contravened a personal order from Hitler that Jungvolk and Hitler Youth members were to attend each National Youth Day and not go to school.

The rolling of the drums and the noisy bugles had been calculated; scarcely any part of the town was without its inquisitive neighbourhood Gestapo spy.

The programme of recruitment was speeded up and it was successful. By 1938, Hitler Youth membership had reached 8,700,000, half of it female. By then there were new slogans on the barrack squares and in the exercise fields: 'The rifle is the bride of the German soldier.'

Hitler's young was not to fight, not just yet. But Hitler had already effectively stolen the childhood of an entire generation.

He had his youth as hard as Krupp steel.

8

To the rousing, thumping lilt of the 'Horst Wessel Lied'
six thousand eager-faced youth swung through the
entrance of the Hitler Youth camp north of Munich.
Their progress took them through the vast centrepiece
of soaring, squat pylons topped by flaming beacons and
giant Swastikas.

The march was past guardhouse sentry-post huts and
khaki tents towards the vast green central enclosure.

The words of the song spoke of triumphant arrogance:

For the last time the Reveille has sounded,
For battle sees us stand in stern array . . .

Then came the fanfare from the boy trumpeters, and
the ramrod-backed ranks were addressed through loudspeakers by the operations leader.

It was by no means the start of the day in this Hitler
Youth camp; already there had been the early morning
route march and the field exercises.

Saturday noon for the six million Hitler Youth in
camps all over the Reich was much the same. This was in
accordance with the Fuehrer's decree: school was to be
for five days a week, Saturdays at least were to be
sacrosanct to the Hitler Youth.

It was not just the parents who were afraid to refuse.
Pressures had been brought on employers to release on
Saturdays their junior clerks and office boys, appren-
tices and all other labour under eighteen.

Hitler had spelt it out: 'In state-created sports and

exercises the young must be moulded into strong, healthy citizens with the right ideals of Nazi manhood.'

However, the object was not to produce strong, healthy citizens for the long jump and the hundred-yard relays. True, in the camps it was possible to see long white lines like running tapes. But for any veteran of World War I their purpose was clear enough – they were the kind that were pegged in the ground at night to guide troops to breaches in front-line wire, to mortar and machine-gun assault positions.

Here, a youth would be taught to outflank a machine-gun post, how to take cover, how to assemble at a position with maximum speed and minimum risk.

There was an outdoor rifle range; there was an ordnance lecture theatre with tables littered with guns and rifle components, with shells and bullets. Weapons were stripped and bisected to show their working parts. And there was the lecture theatre, its walls covered with map-reading charts and tactical diagrams.

A huge black hoarding dominated the camp's green oasis with its constantly hectoring loudspeakers. The message of the boarding summed up as nothing else the main reasons for the camp's existence.

It read: *'Wir sind zu sterben fuer Deutschland geboren.'* ('We are born to die for Germany.')

A British journalist and a colleague had been invited to attend a similar camp at Munchen-Gladbach in north-west Germany, some eighteen miles from the Dutch border. The emphasis on military training was obvious. The reporter recorded:

Presently a company of about eighty boys of eleven years of age arrived. They were in the charge of a squadron leader aged sixteen. He was the most exacting martinet I have ever had the pleasure of meeting. He told us, with disgust in his voice, that although they had had many drill lessons they were still unable to march with military precision. Everyone was agreed on the enormity of this crime. Our martinet friend drilled his squad for a while, and then gave up in disgust. He informed us he would take them to see the 'military' and some proper marching. We accompanied them to the military camp about a mile away. Three thousand soldiers were here, the first time since 1919. By six o'clock that night those little boys of eleven had achieved their leader's life-long ambition, they would march with military precision. There was a smile of happiness and contentment on their faces . . .

A small boy knocked on the door on some errand or other. He was sent outside five times for not clicking his heels as he said 'Heil Hitler', before beginning to speak to his superior officer.

Visitors to Germany remembered the earnest bespectacled schoolboys of twenty years earlier who had looked out unsmiling and pale at a country in humiliation and defeat. But here was a new generation doing its physical exercises in nothing but a black bathing-slip on sunburnt bodies, looking like Olympic athletes.

They were, of course, fuelled by slogans, hassled every moment of the day by ideology expressed in flowery harangues like: 'You were born as Germans; you must live as fighters; you must die as heroes; remember those who fell for the Nazi revolution.'

There would be no let-up at all for Schirach's eager disciples, particularly for those who elected to make a full weekend of it, as many did. A three-day camper checked in immediately after work on Friday and was thankful to go straight to bed.

It was just as well. Saturday began at dawn to the sound of bugles with some thirty minutes of physical training straight after ablutions. The manual for the Hitler Youth, drawn up by SS-Hauptsturmfuehrer

Remold, mapped out the entire day, beginning with the general flag parade a 7 a.m. and taking in such field exercises as distance judging, observation, the harnessing of country features for cover and open-order skirmishing. Then there was a spell in the ordnance lecture theatre – the use and care of weapons, including grenades and rifles, light and heavy machine guns and Minenwerfer. And there were the lectures where the students had to remain alert and sample the official Youth Camp curriculum with such subjects as 'The German Saar', 'The Ruhr and Reparations', 'The Dawes Plan and the Young Plan'.

Although the boys were theoretically free to go home on Sundays, considerable pressure was put on them and their parents to let them stay.

Pastor Kahn, the official chaplain of the Hitler Youth camps, was stung into protest: his job, he reasoned, had become a sheer mockery. He prefaced a long and indignant memorandum to the Reichsjugendfuehrer: 'I can no longer keep silent.'

Schirach took no notice of repeated protests that solely warlike and unchristian activities were being drummed into the boys on the sabbath.

Anyway, by the end of the 1930s it was too late to reverse the process. The physical training and open-air life which converted youths and boys into sun-browned young automatons were ultimately to serve only one real purpose – to build up suitable human material as trained fighters for the armed forces.

On Sunday nights, when it was all over and the tired teenagers summoned their last reserves of strength to march past the pylon gateway again and raise their lilting voices in song, their education in Nazism had advanced more than a little. According to the *Angriff* newspaper, what was emerging was 'the Hitler Youth, a new type, a heroic type, the child and youth who will die for his ideal as the older soldier does in war.'

But the small boys who crept into their homes so weary that they could barely drag themselves up to bed, or answer the anxious questions of their parents, could not expect to be left alone until the next weekend.

Hitler was poaching their souls the other six days as well.

Dr Robert Ley, head of the Labour Front, a former chemist who had been party chief in Cologne, did not believe in being coy. He had written on education:

> We begin with the child when he is three years old. As soon as he begins to think, he gets a little flag put in his hand; then follows the school, the Hitler Youth, the storm troops and military training. We don't let him go; and when adolescence is past, then comes the Labour Service, which takes him again and does not let him go until he dies, whether he likes it or not.

On 23 April 1934, SA-Obergruppenfuehrer Bernhard Rust, former Gauleiter of Hanover, a Nazi party member and friend of the Fuehrer since the early 1920s, had been named Reich Minister of Science, Education and Popular Culture.

Rust, hand in glove with the National Socialist Teachers' League, lost little time in unleashing a sharp, vicious purge on the teaching profession.

For pupils, it provided a luxurious opportunity to pay off some old scores. In Munich, members of the Hitler Youth smashed their way into the apartment of a hated Latin mistress who they considered marked their examination papers unfairly.

The rooms were wrecked, the woman intimidated. Police, when they arrived, were greeted at the door by fresh young innocents' singing sentimental campfire songs. They were wearing Hitler Youth uniforms; the police were powerless to do anything but take a few names.

In the classroom, pupils, bereft of the normal schoolbooks – which had been either banned or removed by teachers anxious for their jobs – clutched *The Awakening of Germany* by a Bavarian teacher named von Fikeschner. On the instruction of Hans Schemm of the National Socialist Teachers' League, it formed the subject of a six-week course.

It taught that the Allies had rubbed Germany's nose in the dust after the defeat of 1918 and robbed the country of its self-respect. The pupils learnt:

> In the hopeless time after the war, there were many parties in Germany which undertook to help the German people if they were only elected and came into power. But amongst all the Germans there was only one who was chosen by fate to lead Germany to the right road. This man is Adolf Hitler.

If all this was considered too heady for the youngest children, von Fikeschner had other suggestions on how they could be suitably amused. It was suggested that a pupil who had a father in the SA should borrow his uniform and bring it to school, so that the class could draw it and become familiar with badges of rank and medals.

There was even a song to accompany the task:

> Not only wear the brown shirt, but obey!
> The Hitler Youth is a preparatory training for the SA
>   and the army!

Some ideological training was decidedly more sinister, offering hints of what the Nazi 'new order' was to mean within a very few years.

A textbook would enquire:

A mentally handicapped person costs the public 4 Reichsmarks per day, a cripple 5.50 Reichsmarks and a convicted criminal 3.40 Reichsmarks. Cautious estimates state that within the boundaries of the German Reich 300,000 persons are being cared for in public mental institutions. How many marriage loans at 1,000 Reichsmarks per couple could annually be financed from the funds allocated to institutions?

In the universities, a relentless programme of suspension, dismissal and premature retirement forged ahead. Prominent among those to go was anyone who had engaged in Left-wing activities, or was 'non-Aryan', or both.

In *The Hitler Youth: Origins and Development 1922–1945*, H.W. Koch revealed:

Within the first twelve months of National Socialist rule, 14.34 per cent of the entire university teaching staff and 11 per cent of university professors were dismissed. These figures obtain their true significance only if one looks at the impact of the dismissals or suspensions on the individual universities. Dusseldorf lost 50 per cent, Berlin and Frankfurt-Main 32 per cent each, Heidelberg over 24 per cent, Breslau 22 per cent, Goettingen, Freiburg, Hamburg, and Cologne lost between 18 and 19 per cent of their teaching body. Famous holders of the Nobel prize were banned.

The purpose of it all was left in no doubt. Hitler's *Mein Kampf* declared:

Education in a general way is to be the preparation for the later army service. The army will then not need, as has hitherto been the case, to give the young man a grounding in the simplest exercises and rules

. . . it should rather change the young man, already physically perfect, into a soldier. The state must throw the whole weight of its educational machinery, not into pumping its children full of knowledge, but in producing absolutely healthy bodies.

The dictum was greeted with almost hysterical eagerness by Hans Schemm, who enthused:

The consciousness that a Lord God lives in heaven, that this Lord God has sent Adolf Hitler to us, that He has allowed us the grace to become a people again . . . ! We will, Adolf Hitler, so train the German Youth that they will grow up in your world of ideas, in your purposes and in the direction set by your will.

For German education and German learning the effect of Nazification was drastic. Curricula were changed and textbooks hastily rewritten or done away with altogether. A British magazine, invited to run a photo-feature on the German schools, showed boys sitting with nothing in front of them but copies of the Nazi party newspaper, the *Voelkischer Beobachter*, which provided them with their sole knowledge of world affairs.

The regime at the mandatory weekend camps was frequently so vigorous that teachers were soon complaining that pupils, particularly those in the Jungvolk, were slumped asleep at their desks on Monday mornings.

Young boys came home at the end of the day with precise instructions. They were to badger their parents for toys that were realistic models of aircraft and tanks. Any parent unwise enough to refuse found that news of the defiance soon reached the teacher. The result, at its mildest, could be a warning. There was even the risk of arrest on the charge of being 'unworthy of the name of a German parent'.

Baldur von Schirach was shrewd enough to realise that the approach of adolescence might well spell questioning and rebellion by the children; the machinery of the Reichsjugendfuehrung must in no circumstances be allowed to relax its grip. At the age of twelve, members of the Jungvolk were scooped out of the main education system and placed in the autonomous Adolf Hitler Schulen.

Here was a highly effective way of moulding the ultimate élite. An entrant basking in the glow of approval from his immediate superiors and local party leaders came under the direct authority of Schirach and Dr Ley.

Successful candidates had, of course, to be superb physical specimens; a searching medical examination by a Hitler Youth doctor led to a high quota of failures. But although combat sports such as boxing, wrestling and fencing were taught alongside the inevitable paramilitary training, Schirach and Ley were looking above all for ideological storm-troopers.

While the girls were taught feminine athletics and domestic science, together with the mandatory National Socialist 'world philosophy', the boys were plunged into an orgy of indoctrination on *German* nationalism, *German* superiority. Their teachers' highly selective view of history had to be absorbed along with a steady diet of sausages, potatoes, sauerkraut and bread eaten in spartan surroundings on plain wooden tables. Beer and tobacco were banned as 'unhealthy'.

On his arrival, the pupil was left in no doubt of his principal lesson from early morning to late at night. The enrolment book – he would be given his own personal copy – contained on its front page the stark phrase: 'The German's body belongs to Germany.'

At the end of the day, the student might have been

misled into thinking that the time had come for relaxation. There was an almost cosy after-supper atmosphere in the school's main hall. There were stirring marching songs and then a school leader appeared for a talk on Hitler's childhood.

Pupils learnt how the Fuehrer lost both his parents, then in a hostile world went bravely by himself to Vienna, to become a painter.

There was a second lecture, this time on the Munich revolt of the Nazis and why it had failed. At the conclusion, the student might have been forgiven for thinking that at least it was time for bed.

It was then that the questioning began. Questions were not asked of the assembled students, but yelled at them. Instant answers were expected.

'What was the consequence of the leader's imprisonment after the revolt had failed?'

The class yelled to a man: 'The consequence was that the leader was able to find time to write *Mein Kampf*, which is the guide of us all.'

'What does Chancellor Hitler want?'

Came the yell: 'He wants to lock up the Godless Communists. He wants to drive out the Jews. He wants a proper government. He wants to give every German work. He wants to help the peasants. He wants an army again. He wants to make the German people powerful again.'

At last the leader cried: 'Boys, to your feet!' Thirty figures sprang to attention. 'Greet the leader.'

Three times came the chorus: *'Sieg Heil! Sieg Heil! Sieg Heil!'*

With flushed faces, thirty grateful boys scattered to their hard dormitory beds.

It was a tough programme, by any standards. But attendance at the Adolf Hitler schools was a prelude; ahead lay the goal of the infinitely more prestigious Nationalpolitische Erziehungsanstalten – National Political Institutes, or the Napola.

No one in their senses would have said so in public, but members of the Napola were apt to look with condescension on the Adolf Hitler schools. After all, the antecedents of the Napola were infinitely older than even the Weimar Republic. They had their origins in the cadet institutes for the training of future officers in Imperial Germany and, more particularly, in Prussia, where they had been founded by King Frederick William I, the father of Frederick the Great.

An attempt was made to emulate the British public-school system with an added militaristic bias. In place of school forms were platoons; the boys indulged in para-military exercises, which might include the capture of a defended foreign bridge or being dropped from the sidecar of a motorcycle unit in unfamiliar territory.

For Baldur von Schirach, the taste of power was to prove sweet indeed. Threats to his growing empire seemed to have been effectively removed. Chief among these, of course, had been the SA. But on the bloody last week-end of June 1934, Hitler, using as a pretext an alleged plot by the storm-troopers to seize power, had struck down Ernst Roehm and scores of his followers. Roehm himself, lodged in a cell in Munich's Stadelheim prison, took bullet after bullet in the chest from two turncoat comrades.

Some 150 other SA leaders were rounded up in Berlin, stood against a wall of the cadet school at Lichterfelde and shot by firing squad on Hitler's orders. To Schirach's fastidious soul it was a distressingly crude way of tying up some loose ends; plainly, power came out of the mouth of a barrel in the Third Reich these days.

Schirach wisely made sure that his legendary energy remained as prodigious as ever, along with the dedication of his Hitler Youth to comradeship and socialism.

On socialism, Nazi-style, he was even prepared to be

lyrical: 'There is no special Hitler Youth for the poor or rich, no Hitler Youth for the grammar school pupil or girl, or for the young worker. Both wear the garb of the community of comrades: the brown shirt of the Hitler Jugend.'

Yet to many, the dedication had something too calculating about it; the tubby, smiling cheer leader with his fleshy, self-indulgent face and middle-class American forebears had never been bawled out on a barrack square. Leaders of the Hitler Youth whose fathers had starved through the lean years had, during one rally in Hamburg, stayed in a cheap hotel, while Schirach had ostentatiously chosen a de luxe establishment on his own.

Such tactlessness was not forgotten. There were also hints of a girlish bedroom and a living-room decked out in white. All this, it was argued, pointed to a careerist mountebank. But the fact remained that Schirach had been talking direct to the Fuehrer since 1933, and it would be foolhardy to be unduly critical of anyone in that position.

As for Hitler, he could scarcely gainsay the devotion of a besotted disciple who could write:

That is the greatest thing about him,
That he is not only our leader and a great hero,
But himself, upright, firm and simple.
. . . in him rest the roots of our world.
And his soul touches the stars
And yet he remains a man like you and me.

Yet there *were* those who were far from being besotted in return. August Heissmeyer, a civil servant specialising in education and now a senior inspector within the Napola, had been in youth movements long before the existence of the Hitler Youth. He was not unduly impressed by slogans and flamboyance; this

70

would scarcely have mattered if he had been without powerful friends.

But he had an ally in Obergruppenfuehrer Bernhard Rust, the education minister, who was firmly of the opinion that Schirach lacked the necessary experience and maturity to train an élite.

Furthermore, Rust had the ear of a man to whom the training of an élite mattered a very great deal. Indeed, it was the central obsession of Reichsfuehrer-SS Heinrich Himmler who, with his bespectacled Mongolian stare and awesome power as supremo of the dreaded black knights of the Schutzstaffel, looked with burning evangelical zeal upon the magnificent Aryan specimens of the Hitler Youth.

Furthermore, Schirach could not afford to forget that the purge of Roehm and the SA had been carried out largely by the killer squads of the SS.

Baldur von Schirach had need of friends.

9

Generalleutnant Georg von Kuechler, Inspector of War Schools, surveyed with approval the confidential report on forty-six-year-old Oberstleutnant Erwin Johannes Eugen Rommel.

The man's military record, by the mid-1930s, was impressive. The Swabian schoolmaster's son had served with dash in World War I and in 1917 received Germany's highest decoration, the *Pour le Mérite*. For some reason, however, his superiors had not considered him to be of General Staff calibre; in the early days of the Weimar Republic he held a string of humdrum positions. True, in 1933, Rommel had been military instructor to the SA and later taught at military schools, but none of this suggested a likely career of brilliance.

There was, however, one quality which marked him out as exceptional. Kuechler was suddenly all attention when he read: 'Oberstleutnant Erwin Rommel is a senior instructor with a particularly powerful influence on youth.'

Hitler had never ceased to remind the Wehrmacht that some of the greatest victories in German military history had been won in the classrooms of the elementary schools of Prussia and had reiterated: 'The Army is to be the ultimate school for patriotic education. In this school the youth shall become the man.'

And what of the youth in Nazi Germany? Kuechler knew that by 1937 it consisted of just a single movement, the vast Hitler Youth with a strength of 5,400,000; a strident, arrogant, precocious leviathan where sport, culture and the Nazi philosophy were handed out with a ruthless efficiency that commanded respect.

But *military* training? For the most part it had been para-military, school-cadet stuff which produced wiry young puppies rather than fierce young tigers sniffing for blood. Kuechler had also heard of some serious lapses in discipline. Even the mildest touch of military-style training led thirteen-year-old boys to imagine that they had outgrown the classroom and their teachers. There were cases of disrespect to officers on the parade ground and truculence to parents at home. Oberstleutnant Rommel's credentials might well be the answer to all that.

Rommel had been senior instructor at Potsdam, outlining to students what he saw as the likely aggressive role of infantry in any future war. When he re-read his lecture notes, Rommel, with traditional Swabian shrewdness, decided to make further – and highly profitable – use of them.

The lectures were swiftly converted into the present tense, pepped up with a bit of colour and skilfully edited for a wider audience. The result, a lively, compulsive read, was titled *Infanterie Greift an* – 'The Infantry Attacks' – and submitted to the Voggenreiter publishing house.

Overnight, Rommel became a cult. Armchair tacticians hailed the book as an infantry manual without equal. But Rommel had been aiming his work at young aspiring soldiers; to them, it came as an inspiration. Equally important, Hitler had read the book and approved.

Rommel was human enough to relish the fame. Above all, he enjoyed associating with young people. From Dresden, he had written to his adjutant in 1931: 'Working with the lads here is a *real* joy.'

Kuechler learnt of other good things. Rommel had been heard to tell a fellow officer: 'I regard it as my job to combat the mood of modern youth – against their parents, against the church and against us too.'

In February 1937, Rommel was assigned to a new post – the War Ministry's special liaison officer to Baldur von Schirach, Jugendfuehrer des Deutschen Reiches.

Schirach's first instinct was to regard the move with enthusiastic approval; this could provide the Hitler Youth with a new prestige and power base. The reality was to be rather different.

Short, wiry Erwin Rommel, a man in the peak of physical fitness and with a lifestyle almost of monkish austerity, surveyed the overweight, oddly effete Schirach with dismay and contempt.

Rommel despised almost everything about the younger man. The good looks, he later confided, were those of the lounge lizard, the charm a little too deliberate. Schirach's easy familiarity with a man eleven years his senior also grated. Rommel longed for an opportunity to put the obese whipper-snapper in his place; it was not long in coming.

For his part, Schirach attempted to mask his growing feeling of condescension towards the blunt, taciturn officer with the thick Swabian accent. Rommel was asked to lunch by the Schirachs.

The result was sheer disaster. Henriette von Schirach, attractive and sociable, did her best to put their stiff guest at ease.

The meal progressed in uneasy silence. At one point, with mounting desperation, Henriette gestured towards the dining-room window: 'Oberstleutnant, don't you think we have a beautiful view of the Bavarian Alps?'

Rommel laid aside his knife and fork and stared icily at his hostess. Then he said quietly: 'Thank you, Frau von Schirach, I'm very familiar with mountains.'

In October 1917, in a brilliant action, Rommel had succeeded in capturing Monte Matajur, south west of Caporetto. At 7,000 feet his booty had been 150 Italian officers, 9,000 men and 81 guns. The episode had brought him his *Pour le Mérite* and up to World War II was the high spot of his military career. Of this last fact, the Schirachs were left in no doubt; Rommel proceeded to lecture them for two solid hours on Monte Matajur. Baldur felt his eyes glazing; his wife made no pretence of interest in military history and struggled to keep awake.

Worse was to follow. Rommel set off on a nationwide tour of the Hitler Youth camps. Always the same complaint reached Schirach: Rommel seemed to regard the youth cadres as potential branches of the junior Wehrmacht that badly needed to be licked into shape. The young men resented being lectured ceaselessly on the storming of Monte Matajur and they did not take kindly to Rommel's ill-concealed dislike of them.

As the son of a schoolmaster, Rommel had been taught that the moulding of young minds was a sacred trust. Children, he believed, should not be fed on fanatical ideology. He was also well aware of how Schirach had ruthlessly intrigued to secure power at the expense of some of other youth movements, which had been forced out of existence with the coming of the Nazis.

A lad of eighteen who turned up in uniform and a large Mercedes and naively confided to Rommel that he felt like a 'commanding general' got short shrift.

Soon Schirach's dislike of Rommel hardened into bitterness and jealousy; the trouble was that the Reichsjugendfuehrer was not clever enough to conceal it. A seemingly trivial incident sealed the two men's mutual dislike. The occasion was a gala theatre performance at which Schirach was tactless enough to seat himself in the front row and place Rommel in the second.

The older man exploded and, moving forward into an empty seat, proclaimed loudly: 'I represent the Wehrmacht and in this state the Wehrmacht comes first.' Chief of Operations Staff at Oberkommando der Wehrmacht (OKW), Alfred Jodl, accurately assessed the situation by confiding to his diary that Schirach was 'trying to break up the close cooperation initiated between the Wehrmacht and the Hitler Jugend by Oberstleutnant Rommel'.

Rommel's open ridicule of Schirach's militaristic pretensions struck hard at the younger man's vanity. Rommel snapped at him: 'If you want to be taken for a soldier, I suggest you go away and learn to be a soldier yourself.' In some heat Schirach riposted that he would lose all influence if he were seen obeying the orders of a drill sergeant.

Schirach turned out to be the loser. The clash by no means blunted Rommel's career. The news of the squabble reached Hitler; the Fuehrer lost his patience and withdrew Rommel. He was selected to act as temporary commandant at headquarters.

There was little that Schirach could do beyond one act of childish spite. He made sure that Rommel was not awarded the golden badge of the Hitler Youth.

But now events on the European stage were dwarfing the importance of who should or should not control German youth.

In that same baroque Bavarian city where Hitler had made his insignificant start as a politician armed with a vague ideology and a posse of young thugs, the now triumphant Fuehrer, a decade earlier the semi-comic central figure of the farcical Beer Hall Putsch, greeted, like a conqueror, the heads of government of Great Britain, France and Italy.

The date was 29 September 1938. The aim of the meeting at Munich was to gain a blank cheque from the Allied Powers to annex the Sudeten area of Czechoslovakia containing around three million ethnic Germans.

The conference, at which the Czechs were not allowed to be present, gave Hitler his way. To underline his triumph, he was soon embarking on a tour of the ancient German cities within the Sudeten border territories; Rommel was given the task of commanding the military escort.

Here was the second fantastic triumph. The previous March, German troops had tramped into Austria, cheering crowds throwing flowers at the feet of the conquerors.

Barely a month after Munich, Foreign Minister Joachim von Ribbentrop was bluntly telling Jozef Lipski, the Polish Ambassador in Berlin, that the time had come for a general settlement between Poland and Germany.

The long baleful night of barbarism was about to descend on a virtually defenceless Europe while the mesmerised democracies watched Hitler's territorial conquests.

For the Hitler Youth, there was still some time left to go on playing toy soldiers at weekend camps. As for

Schirach, he realised that he had lost the battle to gain further prestige for his movement. The only course to secure his own future was to appeal directly to Hitler; after all, those adulatory poems, those years of deference and devotion, must surely count for something.

But events in Europe carried him and the rest of Germany forward on a relentless whirlwind. As it turned out, the next phase of Baldur von Schirach's careerist ambitions was to arrive with complementary speed.

10

Grey skies lowered over Berlin that September morning when Hitler unleashed his monstrous mechanised juggernaut on defenceless Poland, catapulting a million and a half men across the frontier in fulfilment of the code-named *'Fall Weiss'* – Case White.

In public, the Fuehrer had purred peace; in fact the preamble to Case White had contained the memorable sentence: 'Since the situation on Germany's eastern frontier has become intolerable and all political possibilities of peaceful settlement have been exhausted, I have decided upon a solution by force.'

Force amounted to the *Blitzkrieg*, the lightning thrust with entire divisions of rumbling and clattering tanks orchestrated by the animal scream of the diving Stukas. The proud armed forces of the Poles were blasted into oblivion by the Fourth and Third Armies, buttressed in their turn by everything modern technology could provide. And that was formidable indeed: a maze of electronic communications consisting of intricate radio, telephone and telegraphic networks.

There was no escape for troop columns, ammunition dumps. No escape for the Polish government, either; it scuttled from Warsaw to Lublin. The victory was easy, pathetically easy.

Yet in Berlin on that first sultry morning of the Polish assault there was no general mood of elation. The news on the radio and in the newspapers left most of those going to work totally unmoved, even apathetic. The reporter William Shirer wrote:

> Perhaps, it occurred to me, the German people were simply dazed at waking up this first morning of September to find themselves in a war they had been sure the Fuehrer would somehow avoid. They could not quite believe, now that it had come.

The mood had been vastly different in 1914, when delirium gripped the Kaiser's Berlin. This time Adolf Hitler drove from the Chancellery to the Kroll Opera House through deserted streets. Everywhere, it seemed, was indifference.

But not quite everywhere. For the youth of Germany, the ghost of Langemarck still stalked abroad. The call by Hitler and Schirach for unstinted self-sacrifice worked its magic successfully. For the next six years, the appeal would not relax its malign grip. There might be sullen indifference elsewhere in Germany but not in the hearts of the Hitler Youth.

A leading member of the Reichsjugendfuehrung made it very clear that the outbreak of war had seen Hitler Youth totally prepared. He wrote:

> From the experience of the World War was born the idea of National Socialism, out of its armies came the frontline soldier, Adolf Hitler, as its leader. The myth of the sacrifice in the World War of Germany's youth has given to the post-war youth a new faith and a new

strength to unfold the ideals of National Socialism. One of the historic examples provided for us shows that Germany's youth sacrificed their lives for Germany and that Herbert Norkus and all the others who gave their lives did so for a new Germany. This sacrifice had been the most decisive precondition for a revolutionary educational idea and its youth movement.

As far as Baldur von Schirach was concerned, however, self-sacrifice was all very well for the boys and girls of his Hitler Youth but such a stringent philosophy could hardly be expected to apply to him. The unfortunate episode with Rommel, he recognised, had done him no good at all. It would be necessary to reaffirm his loyalty even more strenuously if he had any hope of remaining in favour.

The coming of war provided the only answer. Towards the end of 1939, Schirach bowed to Rommel's half-contemptuous suggestion. A request, duly larded with protestations of eternal patriotic loyalty, was forwarded to Hitler, and he went away to learn to become a soldier.

Plainly, he could not be expected to square-bash with quite the dedication of less exalted souls; within less than six months he had advanced from simple private to full lieutenant.

His time of military service in Nazi-occupied France in 1940 was mercifully brief: neither Schirach nor the Army cared for one another. Besides, Hitler had fresh work for so ardent a disciple; the Fuehrer wanted him in Vienna as Reichsstatthalter – Governor and Gauleiter.

There was no question, of course, of Schirach losing his party offices. He would continue as Reich leader of youth education and remain personally responsible to his Fuehrer for the Hitler Youth. As for the job of Reichsjugendfuehrer, there was an admirable replacement to hand in Arthur Axmann, previously Schirach's assistant.

Schirach's final duty in France was to attend his regiment's thanksgiving service in the cathedral of Notre Dame. Then with considerable relief he exchanged his grey uniform for a grey flannel suit. At the wheel of his black two-seater Mercedes he drove straight to Vienna, to be joined later by Henriette and their four children. The family moved into the governor's palace with its staff of seventeen. The office of governor had considerable prestige in a country rich in cultural traditions; it was all so much more civilised than fighting an unpleasant war.

For the members of the Hitler Youth Schirach had done so much to create, life was to be very different.

The years of innocence were over, that sentimental comradeship of the Jungvolk and its female equivalent, the Jungmaedel. For the youngest echelons of the Hitler Youth, life had not always been hard. A child, tiring of his march, had often been able to depend on leaders to stop for a rest and chat, and sometimes to shoulder packs which were too heavy for an eight-year-old. By forest clearing and lake shore, the children had huddled, singing those touchingly absurd songs about how they would deal with the rotten bones of the Fuehrer's enemies. In the flickering light of the camp fire, it was only too easy to believe they were the inheritors of the earth, part of a great movement that would bring even more glory to Fatherland and leader.

There was a mood of unquestioning trust in the Fuehrer; Hitler pressed the advantage. The magazine *Pimpf* in its issue of September 1940, presented its readers with a prose poem on the gentle heart of the Fuehrer. It read:

Now all German hearts belong to the Fuehrer. His hand is the fate of our Fatherland. All that happens, that determines our present is his will . . . The hand of the Fuehrer leads us.

Then suddenly all those flowery romantic trappings became irrelevant in the harsh realities of total war. One by one, the camp fires burnt low and were extinguished.

Arthur Axmann was soon revealed as a vastly different type from Baldur von Schirach. In the mould of Hitler Youth leaders, he was a reliable and efficient organiser, but also had the knack of gaining the respect of subordinates – which his serpentine, self-indulgent predecessor had never quite been able to achieve.

By the outbreak of war, Axmann had inherited a total of 8,870,000 boys and girls aged between ten and eighteen. But, at a stroke, he faced a command crisis. More than a quarter of the youth leaders were called up for the Army. He hastened to push down the age level of his leaders; now sixteen- and seventeen-year-old boys were in Unterbannfuehrer positions, responsible for anything between 500 and 600 boys.

Inevitably, the previously strict division between Jungvolk and Hitler Youth became blurred; in the last years of the war it was eliminated altogether.

The stiff-backed Wehrmacht did not take kindly to having vast numbers of Hitler Youth thrust on it. The misgivings felt by Kuechler and Rommel about the likely calibre of future officer material from the ranks of the youth movement proved only too accurate.

Dr Bernhard Rust was stung into complaining bitterly that standards of university teaching and scholarship results had grown worse. There was a plague of atrocious handwriting among Nazi youth, who had long adopted the attitude that a neat hand was the mark of a sissy, whereas illegibility marked out an aggressive, fighting spirit.

Disrespect for parents and teachers had long been endemic. Many claims that Nazi-educated boys had been trained in the soldierly virtues from childhood were shown to be hollow. After the Wehrmacht's notoriously stiff tests, a lot were seen as impertinent, undisciplined, lazy and unreliable – the inevitable result of their notorious arrogance towards authority.

For Axmann, it soon seemed that action must take the place of ideology, even at the expense of all that sombre and exhilarating ceremonial. German industry was switched to a war footing; very well, the Hitler Youth would assist in carrying out this transformation.

The government launched an immediate campaign for materials to be converted into munitions. Germans were ordered to turn out their attics, cellars and outhouses for brass, copper, scrap metal, razor blades and bottles. The job of collecting was turned over to the Hitler Youth. Axmann detected an opportunity here of improving discipline.

His various echelons were assigned streets, districts, apartment blocks. The precise connection between knocking on innumerable apartment doors and achieving the superiority and ultimate glory of the Reich must have struck some young minds as obscure; never mind, their orders were, above all, to be scrupulously polite, to salute smartly and then enquire if any of the vital scrap was available. If the reception was unfavourable or hostile, the wide-eyed innocent merely smiled sweetly and withdrew. If his second visit was equally unfavourable, the amiability was allowed to slip a little. But only a little. Persuasion of a more direct character could safely be left to others specialising in such matters.

District leaders were instructed to make it clear to their subordinates that this activity was no mere chore; the future of Germany at war depended on it. One Hitler Youth member recorded:

— is collecting bottles. I see him before me as he is

running from door to door begging patiently for his bottles.

And then the moment when it came to take them to the collection centre. In his uniform, on the back a satchel stuffed with bottles, in the left hand a basket full of them, balanced only by a massive net in the right hand, also full of bottles. And all that beneath a face looking as though through him and his bottles the war must be won.

Under Schirach, the Hitler Youth had remained rigidly male-orientated. Now girls were drafted into the countryside to help bring in the harvest – this was their year's service, the so-called 'Land Jahr'.

Initially, an anxious Schirach had issued an instruction that all members of the Bund Deutscher Maedchen should, because of the blackout, be in before the onset of darkness. This order had been countermanded by Axmann and then quietly forgotten.

Not everyone was as happy as the girls about Land Jahr; misgivings were voiced particularly by parents who complained angrily about their daughters being made pregnant. Pretty city girls were known to disrupt peasant households. The phrase 'Strength Through Joy' inevitably took on a more ribald connotation with a lively little song:

In the field and on the heath
I lose strength through joy.

The party faithful, however, did not waste time on moral considerations. Their view was predictable: the higher the birthrate of pure healthy Aryan babies, the better.

One man, however, was determined that the generation to take over after the war had been won would not result solely from casual sexual encounters. To the racial ideologist Heinrich Himmler, Reichsfuehrer-SS, breeding Aryan children for tomorrow's victorious Germany was a sacred enterprise to be undertaken scrupulously.

With the same punctiliousness which had led him to study in minutest detail the Order of Jesuits and to create a kind of SS monastery in a medieval castle in Westphalia, Himmler now turned with renewed zest to his project of a thriving breeding establishment, the 'Lebensborn', with its cheap private maternity homes.

With the prissy pedantry of a man to whom bureaucracy was in itself a species of religion, Himmler set about drawing up minutely detailed rules for what he saw as a divine mission.

The new SS decree was issued before the war was barely a year old. Its architect proclaimed: 'German women of good blood have the high task of becoming from a deep moral sense mothers by soldiers fighting at the front.'

Then came the small print; the girls of the Hitler Youth had to be of Aryan ancestry as far back as their great-grandparents, free of hereditary disease and more than five feet five inches tall. In addition to signing innumerable forms, composed by the Reichsfuehrer-SS personally, the girls had to sign away all claims to any child that might be produced.

It was a tempting prospect for any young girl, suddenly finding herself whisked away from everyday life in a German city at war. The tedium of an office job could at the stroke of the pen be changed for an attractive furnished log cabin overlooking an Alpine lake. There the newcomer, with her own wireless set and gramophone, would be waited on by smiling SS soldiers serving excellent food. In the evenings, there was plenty of dancing, and the coy little community boasted a cinema.

There was no unseemly haste, no visible pressure. In normal circumstances, a high-spirited young girl of twenty-one might well have resented being monopolised quite so obviously by a fair young man in a black and silver SS uniform whom she knew only by his first name.

In fact, she had no choice; before she left home, Himmler's lieutenants pored over their beloved files and worked out her particular match.

Then came the first instruction: compulsory attendance at the local medical centre. In a few days, the girl would be told solemnly: 'You have been passed fit for your patriotic honeymoon.'

From then on the blond SS escort spent alternate nights with her in her pleasant bedroom overlooking the lake.

If she was fortunate, she would become pregnant in under the permitted limit of six months – failure would mean an ignominious return home and no prospect of further advance in the female ranks of the Hitler Youth.

Then life would continue pleasantly enough at the Lebensborn house to which she was duly transferred, with days spent sunbathing, reading and attending solemn SS lectures on maternity.

Parents who objected to their young daughters submitting to SS studs were either ignored or courted the very real risk of a visit from the Gestapo. As for the Lebensborn experiment, it was extended during the war to around a dozen establishments, including one each in France, Holland and Belgium. At one particular Lebensborn home, in Steinboring, a small Bavarian town, as many as nine hundred children were born.

Young Hildegard Trutz was one of the numerous Hitler Youth members who gave birth to Lebensborn children, then parted from their studs and went on to marry long-standing SS fiancés. Himmler was ready for them, too. Indeed they fulfilled an instruction which he had issued as early as 1936, laying down that 'the SS man is expected to marry, preferably between the ages of 25 and 30, and found a family'. The earlier Reichsfuehrer

SS marriage law of 1931, to which every SS man was bound by oath, gave Himmler the power to veto unsuitable brides.

Hildegard related:

There was a lot of fuss and red tape about our marriage, because we had to get permission. As the children of the SS men were going to be the new ruling class in Germany they had to be very careful that the women were not racially objectionable and had the right sort of physique to produce plenty of children. The marriage permit was only granted after an investigation by the Reich Ancestry Office and a medical examination by SS doctors. I also had to complete my certificate of ancestry . . . We found that my ancestors had all been peasants on their own soil, as far back as 1674.

This document had to be submitted to the office for the investigation of ancestry and they sent me my Ahnenpass, passport of pure ancestry. This was a nicely bound leather book embossed with the rune of life. Then I was examined in the police hospital. They were even more thorough than at Lebensborn. All my measurements were taken and put on a card index and again I had to make a statutory declaration about hereditary dipsomania and imbecility in the family. The SS doctor gave us a talk on planned breeding. He said the ideal German mother should have five children to ensure the necessary number for the nation. On no account should there be long intervals between the births; the number of children should be complete before she reached the age of thirty-five. The children born after that age were liable to be weak and unsuited to their calling as the élite of Germany.

Hildegard and her husband, Ernst, were privileged;

they were eligible for an apartment in the 'Kamerad-schaftssiedlung der SS' – comradeship estate – which had been built at Zehlendorff in the west of Berlin.

The couple married in 1939, with Hildegard in a pretty frock of light blue silk and wearing a myrtle wreath. The ceremony was performed in a living room decorated with garlands and Swastika flags, while a small choir sang:

> You now enter the holy league
> For the Fuehrer and the nation.

But beyond the door of the cosy middle-class apart-ment, with its stained rustic furniture, carved wood plates, painted earthenware and door with carved motto: 'Obedience and dutifulness are the foundations of the nation', lay another world embarking on a bitter war.

For others in the Bund Deutscher Maedchen life was decidedly harsher.

Melita Maschmann was just fifteen when Hitler came to power. Her rebellion followed the familiar pattern: intense contempt for what she saw as her parents' snob-bery and authoritarianism. The sources of rebellion were at hand and one particular slogan of the Hitler Youth appealed to her. This was 'Volksgemeinschaft' – national community. She declared: 'It was a phrase which to me had a magical glow and watching a pro-cession of Nazi boys and girls made me long to hurl myself into the current.' Against the wishes of her parents, who were Nationalists and not Nazis, Melita became heavily involved in the Bund Deutscher Maedchen.

Idealism eventually clashed with the crude realities of the Reich at war. There were precious few slogans now and no talk at all of 'the new Germany'. Besides, war work for Melita was outside the country entirely, in the 'living spaces of the east', to which many members of the Bund Deutscher Maedchen were dispatched to assist in the 'resettlement programmes'. In Poland, the native population was driven out in vast numbers from the Warthegau – those parts of Poland annexed by Germany – and replaced by ethnic Germans.

Intent on a career in journalism, Melita was sent to the Posen area as a press officer. The Hitler Youth leader of the Mark of Brandenburg in charge of the Warthegau Hitler Youth asked her to take over the press work in the new district.

One afternoon in November 1939, she found a town cowed with defeat and despair and hatred of the conquerors. Was this indeed the 'new Germany'? If doubts crept in they had to be stilled instantly. She wrote:

> There was no one among us who was not repelled by the situation . . . But were soldiers being asked whether they would like to make an attack? We thought of ourselves as soldiers on the home front . . .
>
> The feeling of suffocation, which was hard to escape, also came from the decay of the town itself. During the first late autumn when I roamed through it with my senses undimmed it seemed to have a particular smell of saturated clothes, stale bread, unwashed children and cheap scent. One was constantly going down the same dark, narrow streets past tenement houses with flaking plaster, crossing broken pavements in the hollows of which puddle after puddle collected. Children emerged from stinking yards with rags wrapped round their feet, visibly starving. They pursued me in my dreams. During the first winter of the war, Posen was still swarming with begging children, but old people and cripples still held out their hands to us. To begin with I walked past

these hands, without putting anything into them. When an old man fell down in front of me with his face in the snow just as I was about to give him a coin, and remained lying there like a log of wood, I was overcome with horror . . .

. . . Often great mountains of coke and coal, intended for the use of the soldiers, lay in the street. These stores were guarded by patrolling sentries. On many evenings I watched Polish children creeping up to the coal in the darkness and filling small buckets or sacks. If they were spotted, the soldier ran after them firing warning shots, or chased them with a barrage of coke. Any who were caught were beaten. At first my sympathies were entirely on the side of the children. I gave them to understand by signs that they need not be afraid of me, but they mistrusted my uniform. They scuttled back silently into the darkness on their ragbound feet. One afternoon I wrested a girl of perhaps eight from the hands of a sentry. In her fear of being beaten she had let fall her bucket and held both arms folded over her head. When she felt herself released, she gave a little cry and ran away. I had bent down for the bucket. Before the soldier could stop me, I threw it into the bushes where the children waited hidden. The soldier glared furiously at my silver-trimmed uniform coat. He could not make head or tail of my intervention.

In a short time I was describing as potentially naive the 'uncontrolled way I had reacted to this encounter with human misery . . . '

And what of those home-front soldiers with whom Melita Maschmann claimed identity? It was not so long back that the Wehrmacht had sneered openly at the para-military war games of the Hitler Youth; no one had wanted toy soldiers with untried young faces flushed with camp-fire rhetoric.

But all that was changing now. A proud and fanatical Hitler Youth went to war with the rest. Held aloft were the twin banners of rune and Swastika.

11

The spirits of Adolf Hitler soared to match the justifiably optimistic mood of high summer.

Just how staggering the achievements of German Fuehrer and Italian Duce were in mid-1942 could be confirmed by a glance at the map. The Axis writ ran from the northern slopes of Spain to Turkey, and the southern shore from Tunisia to within sixty miles of the Nile. From the Norwegian North Cape on the Arctic Ocean to Egypt, from the Atlantic at Brest to the northern reaches of the Volga on the borders of central Asia the story was almost monotonous as a titanic saga of conquest.

As one military triumph succeeded another, a single call above all remained constant. It came from the Fuehrer as Supreme Commander of the German Armed Forces: '*Advance! Advance!* No pause, no retreat.'

The armies heard it far away in the vast reaches of Soviet Russia: *advance* on the abundant oilfields of Maikop; hoist the Swastika on Mount Elbrus, highest peak of the Caucasus. *Advance* along the Volga, take Stalingrad, then all would be set for the ultimate triumph.

The advance would be on central Russia and Moscow from east and west. The last entrail would be squeezed out of the Russian bear. Truly would the world hold its breath.

Left: Reichsjugendfuehrer Baldur von Schirach in 1934

Below: Hitler's 'young tigers' *(photo: Imperial War Museum)*

Right: Hitler Youth fanfare trumpeters at a Nuremberg rally

Below: The Adolf Hitler March (an annual event) enters Furth

Fürth grüßt den Adolf Hitler-Marsch

Left: Hess, Hitler and Baldur von Schirach at Nuremberg, 26 September 1938 *(photo: Imperial War Museum)*

Below: NSKK leader Adolf Huhnlein chats with Hitler Youths from the motorised branch of the organisation

Left: Student and instructor in a National Political Training Establishment

Below: Reichsjugendfuehrer Arthur Axmann greets members of the Slovakian Hlinka Youth, 16 January 1941

Top: Arthur Axmann conducts army generals around radio training establishment attended by members of the Hitler Youth studying to become army signallers

Above: Grenadiers of 12th SS-Panzer Division 'Hitlerjugend' during the Normandy campaign

Top: Generalfeldmarschall Gerd von Rundstedt inspects 12th SS-Panzer Division 'Hitlerjugend' in Belgium, 1943. *Left to right* Kurt 'Panzer' Meyer, divisional commander Fritz Witt and von Rundstedt

Above: Inspector of Armoured Troops Generaloberst Hans Guderian watches the training of youths as tank drivers

Left: Hitler Youths defend the Reichshauptstadt, April 1945

Below: Nazi soldiers wearing the skull and crossed bones insignia of the 'Schutzstaffel' – SS elite – on their caps were taken prisoner by US forces driving to the Belgian border, crossed by Allied troops 2 September 1944 *(photo: Imperial War Museum)*

Right: Young SS trooper who had been beaten up before surrendering *(photo: Imperial War Museum)*

Below: Hitler Youths amongst prisoners captured in Berlin by the Red Army, April 1945

Elsewhere there seemed little to spoil the euphoria. On the last day of August 1942, Rommel launched his offensive at El Alamein; there was every hope of a breakthrough of his Afrika Korps to the Nile.

Although by now totally obsessed with his situation maps and his role of invincible warlord, Hitler did not neglect the effect of all this on the German people. Above all, the youth had to be kept fully in the picture about the pattern of conquest; they were the ones who would soon be required on the eastern battlefields.

The Fuehrer let it be known that he expected something rather spectacular from Arthur Axmann, who lost no time in contacting the one man who could help him supply it.

While troops of the Sixth Army were poised for what was regarded as certain victory at Stalingrad, Arthur Axmann and Baldur von Schirach – the latter in his somewhat nebulous office as Reichsfuehrer for Education – stood together at a grandiose rally in Vienna to establish the 'European Youth League'.

To the Austrian capital had been summoned representatives of Italy's Fascist Youth Movement, the Youth Movement of the Spanish Falange and the Flemish National Socialist Youth, as well as groups from the Ukraine, Bulgaria and Hungary. With observers from conquered Holland and France, here was an admirable opportunity to demonstrate the awesome extent of Nazi conquest.

But the event had another purpose. Closely monitoring the proceedings in Vienna that September was a certain SS-Brigadefuehrer Gottlob Berger, one of Himmler's pets and, as an able recruiting officer, architect of the Waffen-SS – armed SS.

Berger had earned his spurs at the start of the war when he set up his Waffen-SS recruiting office in a bid to poach recruits from its deadly rival, the Wehrmacht. He had succeeded handsomely.

With Hitler's subsequent approval, Berger was soon establishing a brand-new department for handling foreign recruiting. Funds were made available for the purpose and the process went ahead fast.

Now he had his eye on fresh recruits: there was an agreeable display of talent on show in Vienna. But Berger could never have dreamed just how valuable in two short years the Hitler Youth and its various off-shoots would be.

All was unalloyed optimism that day, with Axmann and Schirach stepping out of their Opel Kapitaen limousine with its black-helmeted escorts and Hitler Youth insignia to the tumultuous welcome from eager acolytes.

For the civilian German population back home in what it fondly believed was the safe cocoon of the cities, the realities of total war were at first blunted. Hitler Youth, however, was left in no doubt of the sacrifices that could be necessary.

Each of the war years was designated with a particular slogan for youth and each year came an indication of just how fortunes were progressing:

1940 The Year of Trial
1941 Our Life, a Road for the Fuehrer
1942 Service in the East and on the Land
1943 War Service of the German Youth
1944 The Year of the War Volunteers

The ultimate change of fortune for the Germans in the Russian campaign, following the relatively soft victories of the conflict in the west, was notable for bringing the realities of the war home to Germany.

The effect on the various echelons of the Hitler Youth was drastic. Groups of the Bund Deutscher Maedchen were among the first to be pressed into action: they were dispatched to field hospitals to entertain and care for the wounded. They helped in state kindergartens and were to be seen on station platforms plying troops in transit with drink and food. The war on the eastern front prompted a call for skis. Hitler Youth members were expected to get skis from their families and it was not long before supply was outstripping demand.

The writer H.W. Koch, whose Hitler Youth unit was part of the Volkssturm – Home Guard – in the closing months of the war, recalled from his own experience: 'Whatever they could not get they simply "organised". And organising in those years of endemic shortage became a fine art as well as a craft which in the end differed very little from actual stealing except that the ends were thought to be unselfish.'

Under conditions of total war, it was inevitable that there would be a scaling down of ideological indoctrination; there were more practical considerations now. Things might, on the surface at least, be going Germany's way in the Soviet Union but the heartlands of the Reich had to endure an ever-accelerating bomber offensive. The rearming of the RAF with four-engined heavy bombers designed in the mid-1930s was stepped up from 1942 onwards. The air war was being carried into Germany and the occupied countries by the Lancaster, the Stirling and the Halifax. And at this time there was the Pathfinder Force, its select crews entrusted with target identification and marking for main force follow-ups.

The call on the ground in Germany was for anti-aircraft personnel. But there was a shortage of manpower; a move was soon on to plunder the echelons of the Hitler Youth and above all of its air arm, the Flieger-HJ. By 1941 it had become accepted that young aviation enthusiasts who had passed two or three months in the general Hitler Youth should transfer to the Flieger-HJ, which in less hectic times had catered for those with a passion for gliders, either models or the real thing. Hermann Goering, as head of the Luftwaffe, had been very proud of 'air-minded' Hitler Youth, fitting them out in a smart blue uniform modelled on that of the RAF.

Now the time for games was over. Former members of the Flieger-HJ, after some rudimentary training from Goering's own *Air Defence Handbook*, were put to man the guns, with the younger ones serving in the communications network of the flak, at searchlight batteries and as dispatch riders. All ages of Hitler Youth were encouraged to be kitted out in Goering's smart new uniform as a Luftwaffenhelfer – Air Force Auxiliary. However, after a searchlight position manned entirely by boys of fourteen and younger was bombed and the entire crew wiped out in October 1943, the younger age groups were banned as Luftwaffenhelfer.

But there was no dispensation from other duties, which meant that mere children were expected to manage motor cycles and ferry dispatches at the height of the bombing. Those Hitler Youth stuck in the cities soon became familiar with every facet of horror in aerial bombardment, from digging corpses out of the rubble, to days and nights dispensing meals to the victims and guarding from looters salvaged property packed high under open skies.

The late summer and early autumn of 1943 were to prove particularly bad for Berlin. Relentless Allied bombing raids brought devastation to the south of the city. For Hitler Youth schoolchildren the pattern became depressingly familiar: into the morning classrooms tramped Wehrmacht soldiers complete with clipboards containing instructions. Pupils were to return home, don their Hitler Youth uniforms and report immediately to places on a list.

Fourteen-year-old Ilse Koehn had lived with her parents in secluded comfort in the northern suburbs, which mercifully at the time had escaped the bulk of the bombing. Then came the day when she was assigned to

Lilienthal School – a temporary shelter for the homeless – where she was to become familiar with the long lines of haggard, distraught faces, their owners clutching their remaining belongings. Somehow, the Red Cross vans were always there with their vast containers of soup, struggling to get past the jostling queues and the eager grabbing hands.

Ilse related:

I finally find a Hitler Youth leader and report for duty, and she leads me through a back door into a huge kitchen. About twenty women are preparing sandwiches around a table. I am told to help. Someone steps out and I take her place. Slice after slice of bread to be buttered and passed on. Butter one, pass it on. I don't know whether I have been here for hours or days. Pick up another, butter it, pass it on. New mountains of bread and butter are constantly brought in. There is no time to look up, no time to think. Quicker, faster, butter it, pass it on. Suddenly: 'Here, you! We need someone at the soup!' and I stand behind a table ladling out soup, seeing nothing but outstretched hands with empty bowls or cups. Soup, more soup, one container replaces another, but the line of people has no end. I'm pushed aside, someone takes my place. Back to the kitchen. Back to buttering sandwiches. I don't see faces, don't know what time of day or night it is. I'm oblivious of everything but the slices of bread that appear in front of me. I butter them mechanically, shove them to the next pair of hands.

In addition, Ilse helped to set up cots, pour coffee, carry blankets and join in the heartbreaking search for young children. All sense of time had long gone; paralysed with fatigue, she barely took in the young man in Hitler Youth uniform grabbing her and saying angrily:

'Haven't you been here since yesterday?'

She could only stammer: 'I . . . I think so,' and scarcely register the barrage of questions about who she was, from where she came.

The Hitler Youth member stared at her disbelievingly: 'Do you know that you have been here for *twenty-six* hours? That's insanity! You are to go home immediately. That's an order! Children should not be allowed here.'

Indignantly, she was stung to reply: 'But I'm almost fourteen! I'm almost fourteen years old.'

Her companion shook his head with mock gravity: 'Old indeed! Go home. Promise me you'll go home. Right now!'

Nazi propaganda, both on the radio and in the press, both in Germany and in the occupied countries, continued to laud the magnificent achievements of Hitler Youth in the cities taking the full brunt of Allied aerial bombardment. There was much talk of noble sacrifice on behalf of the Reich, which would surely emerge victorious in this war, but beneath the surface things were less happy.

The basic creed of Hitler Youth had always laid emphasis on the nobility of violence in the service of a cause. Young Germans had been brought up to take as their models the more brutal types in the SA and the Gestapo, such 'heroes of the streets' as Horst Wessel, whose exploits were built into the myth. And now violence was all round them and they reacted with an orgy of indiscipline with worried the already hard-pressed authorities.

A series of complaints about the behaviour of individual Hitler Youth members, first a mere trickle and soon an alarming flood, began to reach the Reichs-jugendfuehrung. The Gauleiter and Oberpraesident of Hanover, Hermann Lauterbacher, who had been one of Schirach's closest associates as well as a deputy, issued a statement that 'we owe it to the honour of German youth to make a clean sweep of those adolescents who . . . cast a blot upon the reputation of Germany'. The report went on to describe these young people as making themselves conspicuous by 'bad deportment, dirty appearance and extravagant hair style, and regarding it as their mission in life to loaf around the streets'. From Freiburg came accounts of 'a gang of youths who for some time have been waylaying boys returning from school in order to give them a thrashing. At first, apparently, it was a matter of ordinary fisticuffs, but later the youths began to use whips, rubber tubing and truncheons.'

In the worst cases, Himmler muscled in with his SS. There were summary trials and even executions. A report from Hamburg on 20 December 1942 revealed that three juveniles had been condemned to death 'for having committed 19, 11 and 7 burglaries respectively'.

Himmler, in his position as chief of the German police, instructed special patrols – Sonderstreifen – to deal with undisciplined elements within the Hitler Youth. Himmler backed up new measures with a decree that amounted to a drastic curtailment of individual liberties:

(A) Juveniles under eighteen years may not attend cinema performances which finish later than 9 p.m., unless accompanied by a parent or someone acting on the parents' behalf . . .
(B) Juveniles under sixteen years of age are forbidden to attend public dances; those between sixteen and eighteen only when accompanied by a parent or someone acting on the parents' behalf, and must leave by 11 p.m.

Axmann, alarmed at the trend toward anarchy and doubtless more than a little concerned about his own position, went even further. In April 1942, he published a general order forbidding all dancing by both sexes within the Hitler Youth. Eventually the order was modified to exclude properly organised dancing lessons. From then onwards, units of the Hitler Youth could be seen marching to their dancing tuition in close formations, although even then attendance was made conditional on good work at school.

As the destruction by Allied raids spread, bulletins on the German radio were monitored extensively by the British press. *The Sunday Times* for 25 April 1943 reported:

> German industry is going back to child labour to make good manpower losses . . . Nearly 6,000,000 juveniles are working in the factories, but those are not enough. Now children of fourteen may be called upon to work forty-eight hours a week. The law puts no limit to the working hours of children of Jews, gipsies and Eastern workers.
>
> The German radio revealed that the new measures, for all their thoroughness have not met the need. 'The younger generation still available is not sufficiently large to cover the increasing demand for a younger generation trained for the war effort', it said.

As it turned out, there was other work for which the Hitler Youth was already in demand; it was not to be on bomb-shattered streets, ruined buildings or the severely undermanned factories.

Back in the dying months and weeks of 1942, all eyes had turned east to the disastrous turn of events in the snow-covered, bloody shambles of the battlefield of Stalingrad.

The seeds of disaster there had been sewn far earlier, when Hitler outlined his grandiose objectives to press on to Egypt and beyond. For the truth was the Germans lacked the basic war material to achieve the inflated dreams of their Fuehrer. It was not so much the lack of enough guns and tanks; there was not even the means to transport them.

The fatal flaw could have been discerned in the situation maps that Hitler, in his mood of blind optimism, failed to study in sufficient detail. Plain for all to see was the build-up of Soviet forces in the Caucasus and at Stalingrad. The long northern flank of the Sixth Army was exposed perilously along the line of the Upper Don for 350 miles from Stalingrad to Voronezh. To anyone who dared point this out, Hitler indicated the presence of three satellite armies made up of Hungarians, Italians and Rumanians. It all looked fine when outlined with neat little flags on a map table; what the flags did not show was the fighting state of those forces in which the Fuehrer seemed to place an almost mystical faith.

The reality was that the armies were inadequately equipped, lacked armoured power, heavy artillery and mobility. What was more, they were not grouped together but spread out far too thinly.

The portents of disaster had been there; subsequent events did nothing to improve the situation. By late September 1942, Stalin was poised to unleash a million and a half men against Stalingrad and the Don flank.

During the next month, however, it looked to some as if Hitler might be right after all in his determination to stand and fight. There was bitter street-fighting in Stalingrad itself, and at first it appeared as if the Germans were gaining the upper hand. But this was not the victory of the battlefield, it was enervating, time-wasting street-fighting in the rubble of the city, with losses never less than appalling.

Those fighting became exhausted, yet anyone who dared even to whisper a suggestion of withdrawal risked dismissal and Hitler screaming in a fury: 'Where the German soldier sets foot, there he remains!'

As the months wore on, Hitler's obsession with Stalingrad deepened and became steadily more irrational. Then those portents which had been so obvious to many back in the summer became terrifying reality.

Early in November, an overwhelming Russian armoured force smashed clean through the Rumanian Third Army between Serafimovich and Kletskaya, just north of Stalingrad.

By the end of the month, twenty German and two Rumanian divisions were cut off in the appalling blizzard conditions of Stalingrad. Hitler had bit his teeth on the Russian winter.

A succession of appeals to the inflexible Fuehrer fell on deaf ears.

German troops in the Caucasus and on the Don were on the run; by the beginning of 1943 they had withdrawn, leaving behind the doomed soldiers of the Sixth Army, but still came the mad incantation:

> Surrender is forbidden. Sixth Army will hold their positions to the last man and the last round and by their heroic endurance will make an unforgettable contribution toward the establishment of a defensive front and the salvation of the western world.

The resolution and the glory and the agony of the Sixth Army was all over by 30 January 1943 with the radio message: 'Final collapse cannot be delayed more than twenty-four hours.'

Three days later, a German reconnaissance aircraft flew high over the city and radioed back from the grave-yard of Sixth Army: 'No sign of any fighting at Stalingrad.'

The defeat of Stalingrad – of 91,000 half-starved, frost-bitten, dazed and broken Wehrmacht troops – was so total and so devastating that it could not be kept from the German people.

For the first time in this war, a major reverse was admitted; a communiqué read over the radio was preceded by the roll of muffled drums and the playing of the second movement of Beethoven's Fifth Symphony. Four days of national mourning were announced.

For the Germans, the loss of Stalingrad was a hammer blow; they had steadfastly believed until now that their Fuehrer was invincible, that the possibilities of defeat simply did not exist.

But Stalingrad was not the only crisis to be faced. There were also the rout at El Alamein and the British-American landings in North Africa. The setbacks and defeats had robbed the Reich of essential manpower; there was a desperate need to stiffen the ranks of what was plainly becoming a defensive war.

Himmler's recruiting supremo, Gottlob Berger, remembered the young sinewy muscles he had seen at the birth of the European Youth League in Vienna.

All that potential fighting talent looked very much like a rich gift for his Waffen-SS legions.

12

How had they fared, those élite black legions with their uniforms of black, their death's head of silver and their flash which was the double runic 'S' of the pagan German?

A few short years ago, it had been the proud boast of Heinrich Himmler that twenty-five per cent of the total intake of the armed forces had volunteered for service in his Waffen-SS. By the start of 1943, however, the claim was demonstrably hollow; everywhere the figures of available manpower were desperately low. Those who had not already perished in the steppe and tundra of those terrible Soviet wastes were tied down on the northern Finnish front, in Serbia and in France.

Gottlob Berger had a twin task. First, he had to wean the Reichsfuehrer-SS off his fervent dream of a blond Nordic volunteer élite for his Schutzstaffel. The days for that were long past. Once he had surmounted that hurdle, Berger was able to put over his next proposal: the Waffen-SS must resort to a major programme of conscription.

Himmler did not like the idea of an élite consisting of conscripts; but he accepted Berger's arguments – there was no choice.

He insisted, though, on rigid maintenance of SS standards of physical perfection. Berger could afford to go along with this – for the time being.

Plunder began immediately within the work gangs of the Reichsarbeitsdienst – Reich Labour Service. The unenviable job was given to SS-Obergruppenfuehrer Hans Juttner, soon at the end of a storm of protest from parents demanding the release of sons whom they regarded as victims of a press-gang.

Indeed, press-gang methods were at first employed to find the required recruits. In a letter to his father, one indignant Labour Service youth protested:

Dear papa, today I have witnessed the dirtiest trick I have ever seen. Three SS men and a policeman appeared at the camp, demanding that all the inmates register on the Armed SS recruiting roster . . . About 60 men were forced to sign, failing which they were given a reprimand or three days under arrest. All sorts of threats were used. Everybody was frightfully indignant. One or two just departed, even through the window. The policeman stood at the door and would let no one out. The whole camp is furious. I've had enough. I've changed completely.

Such a reaction was plainly bad for morale; protest of this kind had to be stemmed immediately. The SS authorities backtracked. A compromise was agreed on. The youths were to be kept in training for a month or so, then offered the choice of volunteering or quitting SS service altogether. Berger reflected bitterly that this was a fine way of solving the manpower problem, but he had no alternative.

Even those who stayed did not always know what they were doing. Berger later confided: 'They had not known what the Waffen-SS really was, only what their ministers and parents told them.'

One man reflected long and deep on Berger's problems. Arthur Axmann believed he had the answer. It involved taking a considerable risk, and the results of failure would be drastic and permanent.

The Reichsjugendfuehrer requested an interview with Heinrich Himmler.

Fortunately, Himmler was in a pleasant mood, his eyes sparkling from behind his pebble spectacles. He declared: 'By next spring I will have nearly a million men under my command. They'll make a vast army of SS units.'

Axmann reflected: 'One third of them will be foreigners, their fighting capability will be in doubt. More important, no one will have tested their loyalty.'

Such thoughts, naturally, could not be expressed aloud. Instead, Axmann said quietly: 'Reischsfuehrer, I think that I could bring you a division that would be composed entirely of volunteers.'

There was the very barest suggestion of emphasis on the last word; it was necessary to be very careful where Himmler's pride was concerned. He pressed on: 'It would be composed of members of the Hitler Youth born in 1926, it would have a value equal to that of the Leibstandarte.'

Axmann knew that there could be no going back now; he was committed, and it could be the end of him. The Leibstandarte was the personal bodyguard of the Fuehrer, the undisputed élite of the élite. Even to mention it in the same breath as the Hitler Youth was playing with fire.

But there was no hostile reaction. Himmler was positively meek. He said only: 'I must seek the approval of the Fuehrer, you understand. I will let you know.'

As it turned out, events which had nothing to do with Himmler or Axmann decided the matter. The crunch came with events on the Russian front.

It was true that the debacle of Stalingrad was followed in March 1943 by the great SS victory at Kharkov. But the Russians were surging into the Donetz basin and Hitler's predictable order was to stand fast. The spectre of Stalingrad stalked the generals; holding on to the area was an invitation to disaster.

One man who knew this above all was Generalfeldmarschall Erich von Manstein, Commander of Army Group South. In February, he had flown to Hitler's headquarters at Rastenburg in East Prussia in the hope of convincing his Fuehrer that 'shortening the front' would release additional forces for a defence further to the west.

But Hitler had not seen warfare in these terms. He talked to Manstein as if the most gifted of his military men was a raw recruit. The Fuehrer said loftily: 'If one fought bitterly for every foot of ground and made the enemy pay dearly for every step he advanced, even the offensive power of the Soviet army must some day be exhausted.'

Hitler seemed mesmerised by the SS-Panzer Corps,

stubbing the map and saying that only the S~~S~~ [...] able to remove the acute threat of the middl~~e~~ [...] front. The Corps had only recently been esta~~blished~~ [...] Hitler had a new toy and was determined to play w~~ith it~~.

Manstein confided later ruefully: 'Long-term objectives? The Fuehrer displayed no interest in them. All I could do was my best.'

And that, unfortunately, was far from being enough to satisfy Adolf Hitler. The Russian advance hurtled on, approaching the Dnieper. Manstein slashed through the hinge of the advance; the Russians retreated in disorder.

Hitler was to maintain that this told only half the story. The Generalfeldmarschall's strategy had been brilliant, certainly. But it was the three divisions of the SS-Panzer Corps – Leibstandarte Adolf Hitler, Das Reich and Totenkopf – which had spearheaded the operation and recaptured Kharkov.

The casualties were nothing less than appalling. To make Kharkov German again – it was not to be held for long – the SS-Panzer Corps lost 365 officers and 11,154 men.

But Hitler, the man who once proclaimed that 'losses lay the seeds of future greatness' was in seventh heaven. The mineral-rich Donetz basin was secure for the Reich. Stalingrad had been avenged and the policy of no retreat vindicated. The Waffen-SS basked in glory.

Arthur Axmann, naturally, was delighted.

It was mid-February before Himmler was able to inform the chief of Hitler Youth that the Fuehrer had given his approval for the new division. Himmler required that Axmann should work out the details of organisation with Gottlob Berger.

For Berger himself the news was dazzling, and surely, he reasoned, his prospects of promotion must be equally so. His hopes, however, were dashed by Himmler. The Reichsfuehrer-SS was polite but firm. There could be no question of Berger commanding the division, the job he had so desperately wanted. Himmler saw him essentially as a desk man.

It was scarcely a description that fitted SS-Brigade-fuehrer und Generalmajor der Waffen-SS Fritz Witt. He was thirty-six when he was chosen to command and mould SS-Panzer-Grenadier-Division 'Hitlerjugend'. The Wehrmacht nicknamed the division the 'Crack Babies', but came to admire it unstintingly for its tremendous fighting courage.

Tall, muscular, cigar-smoking Fritz Witt – one of the first 120 men to join the Leibstandarte – was a veteran from the Polish campaign, which had brought him the Iron Cross, First and Second Class.

The Knight's Cross had come with the fighting in France. But it had been Russia that had brought still greater honours: the German Cross in Gold, the Infantry Assault Badge and, finally, the Oakleaves to the Knight's Cross. Witt and the rest of the officers and NCOs from the Leibstandarte set about licking into shape volunteers between the ages of seventeen and eighteen, all from the Hitler Youth.

The Reich needed them. The year of 1944 was clearly going to be one of decision in the west. That the Allies would land in France was beyond dispute; only the location was in doubt. Part of the job of stiffening the defences was entrusted to the Waffen-SS. It had, Hitler reasoned, worked miracles before. Why should it not be possible again?

On paper, the resources certainly seemed formidable enough. And they were known to Allied Intelligence. The position of Leibstandarte was pinpointed in Belgium; Hitlerjugend, its running mate in 1st SS-Panzer Corps, was located in Northern France; Das Reich in Southern France; Frundsberg and Hohenstaufen, combined together as 2nd SS-Corps, was in reserve, in Poland.

The war was five years old and could no longer be won by the Germans in an absolute victory. But there were still well-equipped armoured divisions, the cream of the Reich recruits. An invasion on the beaches would face a formidable opponent.

Nevertheless, the fighting calibre of Hitler Youth was so far untested. What account would the 'Crack Babies' give of themselves? Were they really ready for invaders from the sea?

One particular BBC news reader seemed preoccupied that day with the nineteenth-century French poet Paul Verlaine, particularly relishing '*Les sanglots longs des violins automne*' and '*Bercent mon coeur d'une langeur monotone*'. It is highly unlikely that Verlaine ever again had so widely attentive an audience, although it was by no means the quality of his verse which proved so riveting.

The first line about the sobbing violins of autumn was a long-awaited alert to the Resistance fighters in German-occupied France, while the second (possibly chosen by someone with a sense of humour, considering that 'soothing of the heart with a dull langour' was scarcely appropriate) was the final call to arms.

Liberation would begin on 6 June 1944.

From 0005 hours, so went the scheme, aerial bombing of coastal batteries would begin, followed at once by the parachuting of reconnaissance troops, commandos, parachute troops, equipment and glider reinforcements.

In the immediate wake of the invasion on the Normandy beaches, it became obvious to both German and Allied commanders that the vital strategic ground lay to the east.

The British Second Army crouched before the medieval town of Caen while the rest of the Allied forces strained at the leash, impatient to smash through to the open tank country beyond, freeing airfield sites and gaining fighting room before the entire mass of the German Army could be committed to battle.

To a maximum depth of forty miles, the countryside consisted of mainly small fields which were bounded by stout hedge-topped banks, known as bocage.

There were also woodlands and orchards, fractured by high-banked lanes and muddy-bottomed streams, studded with stout stone villages and farmsteads. To the military eye, it appeared an absolute gift: ideal for defence, particularly by anti-tank weapons and machine-guns.

The Germans were to make the most of the opportunities offered by the terrain, filling in the bocage country with well-camouflaged defence posts and gun positions to a depth of six miles. Thus would Hitler's forces fulfil their Fuehrer's sacred task of defending 'Fortress Europe'. The job had to be done by some ten Panzer divisions, which the British and the Canadians were to try pinning down at Caen.

Among them would be the newly designated 12th SS-Panzer Division Hitlerjugend. In the dying hours before D-Day it was on the move.

The tranquil June air was shattered by the deafening roar of 3,000 h.p. Panzer engines and the sharp scream of tank tracks as 12th SS-Panzer hurtled towards Normandy. The Panzer Grenadiers, clutching their hastily applied camouflage foliage, held on grimly to their Mark 4 tanks. Motorcycle combinations and scout-cars arrowed past them, scorching towards what was to become one of the grimmest killing grounds of World War II.

On 5 June, 12th SS-Panzer had been deployed in an area west of Paris and south of Rouen with its divisional headquarters at Acon.

In terms of numbers and hardware, it looked a reasonable proposition. Indeed, the divisional strength was slightly above establishment at 20,540 all ranks, although it lacked 144 officers out of the authorised total of 664. The division could boast one Panzer regiment, which consisted of two tank battalions, one equipped with Panzers and one with Mark IV tanks.

There was an anti-tank battalion, two Panzer Grenadier regiments, each of three battalions, an artillery regiment, an anti-aircraft regiment and scattered support units. At the time of D-Day the Panzer regiment was lacking thirty-six of its establishment of tanks.

But, for all that, something vital was lacking. An illuminating remark was made by one member of 12th SS-Panzer, who stated arrogantly: 'We shall fight like young tigers.' What was wanted, though, was men who could fight, not like tigers, but as soldiers. The reality was that no less than sixty-five per cent of the personnel were under eighteen years of age. An equally frightening statistic was that only three per cent were over twenty-five, and those were nearly all officers and NCOs.

The rank and file of the 12th SS-Panzer came to worship their leaders, hard fighting men whose exploits were already part of SS battle mythology. There were men like SS-Oberfuehrer 'Panzer' Meyer, whose daring methods had earned him the additional nickname of *der schnelle Meyer* – Speedy Meyer. And there was SS-Obersturmfuehrer Michael Wittmann, beyond doubt the foremost tank commander of the war, who during the Russian battle of Kursk the year before had knocked out 30 Soviet tanks, 28 anti-tank guns and 2 artillery batteries.

Blond, tenacious, SS-Obersturmbannfuehrer Max Wuensche, a product of the élite SS-Junkerschule Bad Toelz, was among the high-fliers transferred from the Leibstandarte to take command of 12th SS-Panzer Regiment.

Their task was not simply to fight a war: in a desperately short time they were to mould fighters capable of absolute obedience, total hardness and, above all, the resolute belief that the word 'impossible' had been blasted from the face of the earth.

These were the young men and boys who on the morning of 6 June were transferred from the reserve of the German High Command and placed at the disposal of Army Group B under the command of Generalfeldmarschall Erwin Rommel.

At 1500 hours they were ordered to the area of Lisieux, preparatory to regrouping west of Caen for the counter-attack against Canadian forces.

But the baptism of fire for the Hitler Youth began even before the grim engagement of Caen. The various assembling units of the division enjoyed none of the luxury of air cover. Here were irresistible targets for the RAF Hawker Typhoons, and they did not neglect them. Wave after wave, they came in with a fury of low-level rocket and cannon attacks. Only after darkness did the assault let up.

Discipline held magnificently. The officers were in there from the first, banishing panic and fear from the men under them by organising trench and dug-out parties, while the anti-tank crews hauled the heavy weapons into line. Only when the camouflage netting had gone up in the early hours were the exhausted youths allowed to snatch the bliss of sleep.

The following day brought the first serious crop of problems. The 2nd Battalion of the 12th SS-Panzer Regiment had been held up because the Panzer tanks of its 1st Battalion were stranded without petrol on the east bank of the Orne river. Rommel and his Army Group B fumed with rage. They had envisaged deploying the whole of the division for a counter-attack. Now they could only muster a Kampfgruppe – battle group – under Meyer's command. In all, there were the Hitler Youth units, together with the 21st Panzer Division.

Divisional orders were terse and capable of no misunderstanding: the division would attack the enemy and throw him into the sea. 'Panzer' Meyer, however, gave the order his own interpretation: he decided to take up a covering position, pending the arrival of badly needed reinforcements.

All three Panzer Grenadier battalions were put into the line with two companies of tanks behind each flank. Artillery support was deployed well to the rear. The idea was to prepare an ambush for the Canadian forces pushing out from the beach-heads. But the enemy was not just the Canadians.

The armoured counter-attack with 21st Panzer Division was scheduled for the next day. Meyer received a telephone call from Witt, his commander, who said crisply: 'The British are after Caen and Carpiquet airfield. But we can't just launch an ill-planned attack. We'll wait until 21st Panzer is assembled and then we'll all go in.'

'Panzer' Meyer asked his old comrade: 'When?'

Came the reply: 'Twelve hundred hours tomorrow, and the best of luck.'

13

The relentless punishing salvoes of the Royal Navy's 16-inch guns whistled above the tall towers of the Ardenne Abbey, where Meyer had set up his command post.

He was barely installed before the attack was under way. And his division was not even in place; it was still strung along the Caen-Falaise road! Out there in front was 3rd Canadian Division, ignoring all other units and driving confidently and arrogantly for Carpiquet airfield.

Here was an opponent of a stamp that Meyer understood. It was bred of bravery, above all. But it was the bravery of inexperience. Many of these Canadians were volunteers, fierce individualists from farming stock who had handled firearms almost from the cradle. What was more, they were superbly equipped, every bit as aggressive as their SS partners and they did not give a damn.

Here was a splendid opportunity for the Germans to mow down the lot.

One of the best chances came when a Sherman rumbled to a halt and there was the Canadian commander, standing upright in his turret, lighting a cigarette. Meyer's field-glasses even picked out the man wincing as the smoke was blown into his face.

Meyer gasped: 'Doesn't the idiot know they're on top of us?'

For a moment, Meyer sweated. Here he was, only a Regimental Commander taking part in an Army Corps exercise, proposing to take a major step without asking questions or awaiting instructions.

He shouted: 'Hold your fire! Nobody is to fire without my orders!'

Then he clattered down the stone steps of the abbey tower, making for the courtyard where Obersturmbannfuehrer Wuensche had established his CP. Quickly, he outlined the position: the Canadians were obviously making for the airfield. The orders from on high had been that they were to be stopped.

Meyer let them keep on coming; right into a trap.

Swiftly, Wuensche passed orders to his tanks hidden in the grass beyond.

'*Achtung! Tanks advance!*'

And all at once their fire-power spoke; the slaughter of the Highlanders of the 3rd Canadian Division had begun. The tanks were out of the orchards now, firing as they came. The Highlanders began pulling back to the village of Authie and a knot of Canadian prisoners shambled into the abbey's grounds.

The scrap was still continuing, and it was not Meyer's way to keep out of the action for long. Suddenly the CP began to lose its charms; it was time he was with his men, the tank crews – sinister in their black leather clothing – who had lowered themselves into turrets daubed with the names of their girl friends.

Once again he flew down the steps, making for the 3rd Battalion, which was hammering the retreating Canadians with commendable ferocity.

He never made it. The Canadian shell exploded right in front of his motorcycle, slicing off the front wheel, which catapulted into the air. Then a giant fist was hitting him and punching him off the saddle.

When Meyer came to he found himself staring straight into the frightened eyes of a Canadian private. With shells exploding around them, movement of any kind was out of the question. Instead, both men were riveted to the spot, heads pressed to the heaving ground. Then came a merciful break in the bombardment. For the moment, German and Canadian stared at one another. Meyer gave the barest suggestion of a shrug. Then he was on his way, pounding towards the battalion. The Canadian waited a short time to chart Meyer's direction, then headed the other way.

By now the battle was over. Its awesome cost was only too apparent; the abbey grounds were littered with wounded and dying Hitler Youth. Meyer's 2nd Battalion was without its commander, who had been killed in action. Most of its company commanders had perished also or were severely wounded. Heavy losses were reported by 3rd Battalion, and most of the armour had been wrested from the tank detachment.

But it had long been accepted that heavy casualties

were the hallmark of an élite Waffen-SS division. Emil Werner, of the 25th Panzer Grenadier Regiment, described bitter fighting elsewhere on 7 June:

. . . We stormed a church where snipers had taken up positions. Here I saw the first dead man from our company, it was Grenadier Ruehl from headquarters platoon. I turned his body over myself – he'd been shot through the head. He was the second member of our company to die. Dead comrades already and we still hadn't seen any Englishmen. Then the situation became critical. My section commander was wounded in the arm and had to go to the rear. Grenadier Grosse from Hamburg leapt past me towards a clump of bushes with his sub-machine gun at the ready, screaming: 'Hands up! Hands up!' Two Englishmen emerged with their hands held high. As far as I know, Grosse got the Iron Cross, Second Class, for this.

A counter-attack against the Canadians was considered. It was swiftly rejected. True, the Canadians had either been wiped out on the spot or driven back with heavy tank and infantry losses. That their operation had been ruined was no overstatement. But they had not disintegrated; the drive for Carpiquet airfield would go on.

As for the 'Crack Babies' division, it had been blooded in battle and Meyer could only concede that it had done well. But how long would its ranks survive? Eventually there would have to be a counter-attack, before it was too late.

General Geyr von Schweppenburg, commander of Panzer Group West, was a supreme realist. He knew that the war was lost; if the German High Command insisted on continuing with the lunacy, then the only course was to hit the enemy as hard as possible and hope to survive a little longer.

So he climbed wearily to 'Panzer' Meyer's tower observation post for the SS man's situation report. But he was soon brushing it aside, impatient with the fanatical SS talk about 'ultimate victory'.

To argue would be a waste of breath. The General contented himself with the cynical comment: 'My dear Herr Meyer, this war can now only be won by political means.'

Still, there would be one last major effort – a bid to break through to the coast with three armoured divisions. Out of Caen, 21st Panzer would attack on the right, with 12th SS in the centre and Panzer Lehr Division on the left, near Bayeux.

Schweppenburg announced: 'The operation will begin as soon as Panzer Lehr reaches the front and has deployed.' He stared levelly at Meyer, adding: 'You must understand that, win or lose, the divisions will be burnt out by the time it's all over. We won't be able to do it again.'

Any joy at the thought of a counter-attack was short-lived. The initiative was swiftly seized by the British and Canadians, appearing in front of the German lines.

The three divisions were gradually edged over on the defensive. Meyer received a summons to the headquarters of his Corps Commander, SS-Oberstgruppen-fuehrer und Panzer Generaloberst der Waffen-SS Josef 'Sepp' Dietrich.

Under the influence of this former tobacco factory foreman and petrol pump attendant, the Leibstandarte had developed into one of Germany's finest units. Of Dietrich's record in Russia, Joseph Goebbels had written: 'If we had twenty men like him we wouldn't have to worry at all about the eastern front'; and Hitler himself had enthused: 'He is a man who is simultaneously cunning energetic and brutal . . . And what

115

care he takes of his troops!'

Now this paragon was admitting to Meyer: 'I'm scraping the bottom of the barrel. I've thrown in my last reserves.' Dietrich lapsed into the sort of coarseness that habitually laced his conversation to officers and men alike.

'They want to defend everything, these arseholes!'

Meyer did not need to have this outburst explained. Dietrich, the man who had started as a trooper in the 1st Uhlans under the Kaiser and become commander of 6th Panzer Army, meant the German High Command.

SS-Obersturmfuehrer Michael Wittmann was not given to defeatism; his implacable devotion to the SS cause flew in the face of all reason. Certainly, Germany could still win the Battle of Normandy. Had not the Fuehrer guaranteed it?

On the afternoon of 13 June, Wittmann and his old, battle-experienced gun-layer, SS-Rottenfuehrer Woll, another holder of the Knight's Cross, worked their way in a lone Tiger tank toward Hill 213 north of Villers Bocage, which lay directly west of Caen and the airfield at Carpiquet.

Around one o'clock, emerging from a small wood, he spotted, to his astonishment, scores of British tanks rumbling along the road below. A mere reconnaissance unit? There were far too many of them for that. In fact, Wittmann was looking at a leading brigade of the British 7th Armoured Division, Montgomery's old 'Desert Rats'. It consisted of 22nd Armoured Brigade, including the 8th Hussars and the Royal Tank Regiment.

A German Tiger was, of course, more than equal to dealing with a British Cromwell, but just how many Cromwells were there? The sight of the almost leisurely progress of the British infuriated Wittmann. He had a sudden desire to teach them not to count their chickens prematurely.

116

Down towards the long line of stationary half-tracks rumbled the Tiger, its 88-mm cannon spitting the message of death. Half-track after half-track erupted. The final tally astonished even Wittmann: twenty-five Desert Rat half-tracks had been dispatched and the whole brigade robbed of its advance.

One Cromwell was ill-advised enough to take up the challenge. The 75-mm shell, fired at close range, resembled a tennis ball bouncing off a racket. Moments later it was a blazing wreck, the survivors scrambling frantically for safety.

The battered brigade began to fall back towards Villers Bocage, with a dozen Cromwell tanks seeking to cover the retreat. Now Wittmann was no longer alone; the four remaining Tigers of his detachment joined in to finish off the tanks of the Hussars. Soon a further eight Tigers were on the scene, and the British were fighting desperately to hold the village. Wittmann was just beginning to enjoy himself when the shell ripped into the right track of his Tiger. In the rubble of the wrecked houses, British troops, armed with the spring-powered anti-tank bazooka, the Piat, waited with relish for this temptingly easy target.

Wittmann saw no point in hanging about; it was an almost criminal waste of a Tiger, but at least he had successfully stopped the advance of an entire British brigade.

Opportunities for adventures of this kind, though, were becoming few and far between. A more accurate account of the nature of the fighting at Caen for 12th SS could be gathered from the somewhat fevered prose of an SS war reporter writing for the magazine *SS-Leitheft*:

Thousands of aircraft, rolling barrages of the batteries, masked tank attacks hammered them in with bombs and shells. The earth heaved thunderously. An inferno was unleashed. But faith was the strongest support of courage. Smeared with blood, covered with dust, gasping and fighting, doggedly dug in the earth, these youths brought the Anglo-Americans to a halt.

But there was the cost.

SS-Oberschuetze Hans Matyska felt that he had earned his lunch. His boss, Brigadefuehrer Witt, had been driven safely to his château HQ and there was no reason why there should not be a short lull.

The British artillery spotter aircraft looming suddenly overhead put paid to that. Matyska, a veteran who had come from the Leibstandarte to 12th SS-Panzer, had a sudden presage of disaster. He commented to the Unter-scharfuehrer at his elbow: 'I don't like the look of that. Let's get something to eat under cover.'

But all thoughts of pea soup with sausage were banished as with a mighty roar the 16-inch naval shells from the two British battleships stationed off the Normandy coast ripped into the air. The first salvo hit the ground beyond the château; it was odds-on the next would be more accurate.

Brigadefuehrer Witt came running out of the house, his staff officers fumbling for their helmets. Witt yelled: 'Over here, Matyska. Into the trench!'

The Oberschuetze streaked from the protection of a stone wall, arrowing in on the trench like an Olympic sprinter. The next salvo sliced into the château. And there was a terrible silence. Matyska stared for what seemed an age at the twisted pile of staff officers; the sight of their entwined bodies seemed to hold him like a vice. Then at last he struggled free, in the process pushing aside all that remained of thirty-five-year-old Brigadefuehrer Fritz Witt.

The Division's Chief-of-Staff Herbert Meyer (no relation to 'Panzer' Meyer) was terse with his news when he summoned the latter to the wreck of the château:

'Our Divisional Commander was killed half an hour ago. Corps has commanded that you take over the Division.'

Sepp Dietrich's comment on hearing the news was not only a tribute to Witt but a vivid illustration of the Waffen-SS credo in war: 'That's one of the best gone. He was too good a soldier to stay alive for long.'

Kurt Meyer too was a good soldier. But he desperately wanted to live.

14

'Panzer' Meyer's inheritance was a bleak affair.

By 1 July 1944, the losses of 12th SS-Panzer Division were severe indeed. The British VIII Corps had pressed it back to the western suburbs of Caen with 26th Panzer Regiment reduced to mere battalion strength, its tank regiment virtually wiped out and most of the auxiliary troops, including the engineer battalion, annihilated.

North of Caen, the Panzers of the Hitler Youth had been among the worst sufferers; there were shortages of petrol, ammunition, equipment. Hitler's orders remained inflexible: 'Caen is to be defended to the last bullet.'

Meanwhile, the Canadians were poised to attack Carpiquet, whose airfield had been converted into a formidable last bastion of the Caen defences. It was held precariously by a flak battery of Hitler Youth, elements of the 26th Panzer Grenadier Regiment and some fifteen tanks.

Rocket-firing Typhoons had taken care of some forty other tanks which attempted to engage. The frail forces at the disposal of the Germans had as opponents the

Canadian 8th Infantry Brigade plus a battalion of the Royal Winnipeg Rifles, supported by tanks of the Fort Garry Horse and flail tanks of the British 79 Armoured Division.

Nor was this all. The Germans had also to contend with the concentrated firepower of 428 guns and the warships, including 16-inch guns of the battleship *Rodney* and the monitor *Roberts*' 15-inch guns.

The effect on the German armour was devastating. Meyer was unable to allocate more than two or three tanks which had been concealed in the aircraft hangers. The Grenadiers crouched ready for the fray in sturdily constructed underground blockhouses.

The thunderous bombardment erupted with the first blush of dawn. Canadians in the nearby assembly area of a forest near Marcelet were at the receiving end of a fierce retaliatory barrage, and at the airfield the 88-mm guns waited. Carpiquet village was subjected to a merciless bombardment which served to pin the Canadians down. Neither was the airfield going to prove an easy proposition for the Allies. Here were fifty teenage SS Grenadiers, supported by the Tigers of Obersturmbann-fuehrer Maz Wuensche.

The young Grenadiers – children forbidden to smoke and given sweets along with milk, which took the place of their elders' beer – were the sole survivors of a whole battalion. Many of them scarcely knew how to shave; but they knew all about fighting.

When it came to self-defence this proved just as well. For now the Hitler Youth was facing not simply Canadian soldiers, but a roughneck breed of French-Canadians prepared to fight at close quarters with knives. Their ferocity had been fuelled by reports that the Germans were executing Canadians by tying them to posts and using them for bayonet practice.

'*Caen is to be defended to the last bullet.*' Bitterly,

'Panzer' Meyer reflected that he knew only too well what this meant. It would be the death of his division.

Meyer went to the airfield to see for himself what was going on. The Winnipeg Rifles were edging cautiously towards the positions of the Grenadiers. If they expected trouble, there was disappointment. An ominous silence shrouded the battlefield. The Canadians left the protection of the woods and were approaching one of the hangers where Meyer lurked with his teenage infantry. Then, all at once, the young Grenadiers were out, crouching low and firing from the hip. Those men of the Winnipeg Rifles who had not been cut down turned and ran, seeking the safety of the woods.

The débâcle of the Canadians was the sort of incident to put heart into more than one member of 12th SS-Panzer. But if there was any euphoria it was short-lived.

On the right of Kurt Meyer's front, matters were in the hands of 16th Luftwaffe Field Division, which itself was an illustration of how desperate things had become. Men who were totally ignorant of infantry warfare – combed out ex-air and gun crews – frequently faced the fire-power of the enemy in a state of total bewilderment. Their use to 'Panzer' Meyer was precisely nil; in fact, they were a dangerous liability.

Slowly but surely 12th SS-Panzer Division Hitler-jugend had to pull back.

Nevertheless, the fanatics of the SS around Caen were worrying the Allies. Optimistically, General Bernard Montgomery had hoped to seize the town within twenty-four hours of the D-Day landing. So far, the British reasoned, there had been a mere softening-up of the enemy. The time for such gentle tactics was past. If the Germans could not be sliced to defeat on the ground, then they would have to be smashed to oblivion from the air. General Miles Dempsey, commanding the 2nd

121

British Army, to which the Canadians belonged, turned to the Royal Air Force to help overcome the fanatical resistance of the SS.

The RAF proceeded to bomb Caen to death.

First the massive guns of the battleship *Rodney* hurled twenty-nine shells at a distance of 25,000 yards on to the key hill at Point 64, where the roads from Epron and Lebisey converged before running down to Caen. Then, through the last glowerings of daylight on 7 July, came a massive shot of adrenalin to the British troops who waited so tautly for zero hour. The sudden hum that they heard from the north swelled into a mighty, terrifying roar.

It came from 467 four-engined bombers, which appeared over Caen to drop 2,560 tons of bombs on the northern edge of the city. On they flew into the black curtain of anti-aircraft shell bursts, glittering at lower levels with probing streams of tracers.

Then the bombs fell, and the ground trembled as spout upon spout of smoke and flame leapt up from the ancient city. But still it refused to die. The German forces had slung a formidable defence line across the approach to Caen. A series of villages, with steel and concrete strongpoints, had been transformed into what was virtually a single underground fortress line, which had so far remained intact.

Then Caen was at the mercy of the massive British artillery barrage; the Germans were ready and in strength, with the arrival of the infantry. A Panzer Grenadier wrote in his diary what it was like to contend with the British:

From 6.30 to 3.00 a.m., again heavy machine-gun fire. Then Tommy attacks with great masses of infantry and many tanks. We fight as long as possible but we realise we are in a losing position. By the time the survivors try to pull back, we realise that we are surrounded.

And all the time the plunging Allied fighters and medium bombers kept up the relentless pressure on enemy strongpoints, gun areas, headquarters, forming-up places, bridges, roads and railways. The *Rodney* was active too, sending 16-inch shells among thirty-five Panzers about to enter the fray.

Caen was soon held on the right by an infantry division which had replaced the 21st Panzer Division, while in the centre was all that remained of the Hitler Youth. The order from the Fuehrer was still the same: 'Not a yard of ground is to be yielded.' 'Panzer' Meyer did his best. The thinning ranks of 12th SS-Panzer dug down in the village of Buron, eager to fight to the death – and it took most the day to grant the wish of the Hitler Youth. Again and again, through the smoke and the rubble, the Panzers rumbled into the bloody fray, only to be blasted at point-blank range. A single Canadian 17-pounder anti-tank battery claimed to have destroyed thirteen Panzers.

Meyer's men were falling everywhere, and the cellars of his abbey headquarters ran with the blood of his wounded teenagers. Most of his officers were dead or wounded. Soon he knew that the useless right flank would disappear altogether. For the first time, he admitted that he was heartily sick of this war. Later, he was to write: 'The fresh, blooming faces of a few weeks ago have become hollowed out and grey; the boys' eyes are already dead . . . We were meant to die at Caen.'

On 9 July 1944, 'Panzer' Meyer, commander of the division which bore the name of his Fuehrer, proceeded on a course of action which once he would have found unthinkable. He committed disobedience and ordered the evacuation of Caen.

His achievement, by any standards, had been formidable.

Montgomery's plans to have Caen by 7 June had been thwarted. It had taken over a month for the British to cover a mere eight miles; a devastating setback which the chair-bound strategists, poring over their maps, would have considered impossible.

But the cost proved virtually unbearable to the Germans. Although Caen had been held for thirty-three days and reduced to rubble, twenty per cent of the teenagers were dead and forty per cent wounded or missing.

The 12th SS-Panzer Division was a mere name. But it had not done with Normandy yet.

Caen, the slammed door which had blocked British forces debouching on to the rolling plains sweeping to Paris, had been blown open.

By 26 July, the forces of General Omar Bradley had broken through the German front at St Lô, south-west of Caen on the River Vire. Four days later, the newly formed 3rd Army of General George Patton, racing through the gap, reached Avranches, opening the way to Brittany and to the Loire in the south. Generalfeld-marschall Hans Guenther von Kluge, Commander-in-Chief West, notified Hitler's headquarters: 'The whole western front has been ripped open . . . the left front has collapsed.' The Fuehrer stormed and raved at what he termed defeatist talk; Kluge's reward was dismissal. By the middle of August all that was left of the German armies in Normandy was locked in a narrow pocket around Falaise and Argentan to the south-east.

Suddenly, to the 500 surviving teenage SS, the little village of Falaise became the most important place on earth. On their young shoulders lay the fate of 100,000 men.

As if he did not have enough problems already, 'Panzer' Meyer had to contend with a dive-bomber raid on his car and a resulting head wound. He later recalled:

My knees were trembling, the sweat was pouring down my face and my clothes were soaked with per-spiration. It was not that I was particularly anxious about myself, because my experiences of the past five years had accustomed me to the fear of death. I was afraid because I realised that if I failed now, and I didn't deploy my division correctly, the Allies would be through Falaise and the German armies in the West would be completely trapped. I knew how weak my division was and the task which confronted me gave me at that time some of the worst moments I have ever had in my life.

There was worse, far worse to come. The Germans had, despite their outward show of arrogance, at last fallen victim to the death-watch beetle of despair.

Meyer's Grenadiers, with their two remaining tanks, were rock hard; the men of the 89th Infantry Division were not. Suddenly, there was blind uncontrolled panic and the infantrymen poured down the Falaise road, streaking past the SS. Meyer, unarmed except for a rifle, was left alone with his driver. Whatever happened, this distraught mob had to be stopped and sent back. Otherwise they would all be finished.

Meyer shakily lit a cigar to steady his nerves. Then he stood square in the battle-littered road, daring those fleeing to mow him down. He bawled: 'Are you going to leave a divisional commander alone to fight the enemy?' Shame-faced, the bulk of the infantry returned to their positions.

Wryly, Meyer could not help remembering the days when he used to toss grenades at the feet of those who were reluctant to advance. Now he was reduced to begging for precisely the same thing. Well, there was little point in making those sorts of comparisons now. The end was only a matter of time, anyway.

On the Allied side, the call was on to close the gap, to snap the trap once and for all. It was a dive-bombing offensive of epic proportions, devastatingly cruel even by the standards of total war. All night and all the following morning it raged, the Spitfires strafing a small triangle formed by Falaise and, to the east, the villages of Trun and Chambois.

The Typhoons had already been hard at work, indulging in their favourite tactic against long streams of enemy vehicles. This was to seal off the column's front and rear by dropping a few bombs with pinpoint accuracy. Thus a desperate enemy was imprisoned on a narrow stretch of dusty lane. The transports were frequently jammed four abreast, while rocket and cannon attacks pressed the advantage with maximum ruthlessness.

Those armoured cars and tanks which attempted to escape with detours across the fields were soon spotted by the Typhoon pilots; the runaways suffered the same fate as their comrades in the highways and lanes.

No sooner had the Typhoons withdrawn from the killing ground than the Spitfires raced into the attack. Trucks, staff cars and lightly armoured vehicles all fell victim. The Tigers, of course, were of sterner stuff; the cannon shells bounced off their tough armour-plate. But this did not stop the deadly waves of assault.

RAF Wing Commander 'Johnnie' Johnson, who had led the Western Allies in victories against the Luftwaffe with thirty-eight kills and escorted more than fifty American bombing missions over Germany, recalled at the end of the war: 'As soon as the Spitfires had fired all their ammunition, they flew back at high speed to their airfields, where the ground crews worked flat out in the hot sunshine to rearm and refuel the aircraft in the shortest possible time.'

On the ground, all was panic-stricken chaos, with cars, heavily laden with officers' gear, honking their horns in a desperate bid to clear a path through the shattered lorries, and cannon shells slamming into the ammunition trucks. And somewhere in the centre of this bloody mess, Meyer suddenly bumped into an old comrade, SS-Obergruppenfuehrer Paul Hausser, commander of 7th Army, a distinctive black patch covering the socket of the eye gouged out at the Battle of Moscow.

Hausser squatted in a ditch, shouting his planned next move above the appalling din. He proposed that the remnants of his five armoured divisions, led by the Leibstandarte, would make a desperate bid to break through the British line at Chambois on the River Dives, well to the east of Falaise.

And Meyer's role? He would attach himself to the infantry of 3rd Parachute Division. The 3rd, the SS and various infantry divisions would try to break out near St Lambert, north-west of Chambois.

The plan reckoned without the awesome force of the Allied fighter bombers. Every move by SS-Leibstandarte and SS-Das Reich was frustrated by the rain of shells on the stalled tanks.

The punishing Allied fire made no distinction between ranks; officers and men alike ran the same gauntlet of death in their desperate attempt to reach safety. Among the prisoners of war were a corps commander and two divisional commanders. On foot and in small groups of armoured vehicles, everyone frantically sought their way out of a man-made hell.

One of those who made his bid to escape was Untersturmfuehrer Herbert Walther, a member of the Hitler Youth since he was eleven years old who had volunteered for the Waffen-SS at eighteen. At Meyer's side at Caen, he had won the Iron Cross, First Class. In terms of this war, that made him a battle-hardened veteran.

Walther recalled what happened to him as the pincers closed on the Falaise pocket, and he made his bid to escape:

My driver was burning. I had a bullet through the arm. I jumped on to a railway track and ran. They

127

were firing down the embankment and I was hit in the leg. I made 100 metres, then it was as if I was hit in the back of the neck with a big hammer. A bullet had gone in beneath the ear and come out through a cheek. I was choking on blood. There were two Americans looking down at me and two French soldiers who wanted to finish me off.

But luck was with Herbert Walther that day. An American bandaged the leg and he was driven away on the bonnet of a jeep. Eventually his leg was reset; thirteen bullets had been removed.

Elsewhere the Hitler Youth was in headlong flight; panic had taken on the dimensions of an infectious disease.

By midnight, Meyer and a clutch of men from various units had sped to the Dives. Contact with any other forces was out of the question. All the bridges were in enemy hands.

Appalled, Meyer watched wave after wave of Germans being cut down as they attempted to cross the river. From the direction of St Lambert could be heard the sound of heavy gunfire. Had there been a break-through? It turned out to be minor; there could be no question of his pathetic little group striking out.

There was only one way across that cursed river: to swim it. Meyer slipped into the blood-red water, where the bodies were floating downward on each side. Five minutes later they had made it, but Meyer sensed that some of the two hundred with him were likely to prove mixed blessings.

He looked with contempt at some of the Hitler Youth round him who had flung away their weapons.

Meyer snapped: 'If you haven't a gun, find one. There are plenty of dead lying around.'

This seemed to put new heart into the waverers. Within half an hour, officers and men, having crawled about the field, secured what they could from the corpses of their comrades.

The ragged force with its makeshift weapons moved towards the Trun-Chambois road, and there were the Shermans. For some reason that no one could subsequently understand, the tanks ignored Meyer and his little group; maybe, somebody suggested, in the confusion they had been taken for Canadians.

All at once, exhaustion, total and crippling, struck Kurt Meyer, turning his legs to foam rubber. He was no longer capable of coherent thought, let alone coherent command. Ragged, wounded and exhausted, one of the Waffen-SS's hardest men allowed himself to be led like a child to 1st SS-Panzer Corps HQ.

Sepp Dietrich stared at him in open-mouthed astonishment. He could only gasp: 'But Kurt, we thought you were dead.'

Many were. The total number of German dead and wounded that stained the green countryside of the Dives valley will never be known, although figures of between 10,000 and 15,000 have been estimated.

As for the Hitler Youth, Meyer had seen his division wasted away at the Battle of Caen, with 10,000 casualties among his seventeen and eighteen-year-olds. Twenty-one of his commanders were dead, wounded or captured.

And as if this was not enough, the teenagers were destined to face yet another enemy besides the Americans and the Canadians. Just before 12th SS-Panzer reached the next great riverline, the Meuse, they ran slap into determined bands of Belgian guerrillas. The partisans had mined the roads; young men screamed as a series of explosions sliced off their legs. The partisans were not soldiers and had none of the soldier's code of honour when it came to fighting. They shot their opponents in the back or leapt on them and slit their throats.

Meyer urged the survivors on. He knew that before long the pursuing Americans would be breathing down their necks. Those the partisans had been unable to kill would fall victim to the Shermans, which there were no longer the resources to resist.

A mere 600 Panzer Grenadiers and a handful of vehicles! Ahead loomed the last waterway of the Meuse. 'Panzer' Meyer's reaction was a predictable one for a veteran of five years' war in two continents and a score of countries: he would stand and fight.

For thirty-six hours, in and around the Belgian hamlet of Durnal, Meyer and the Hitler Youth managed to hold the Americans at bay. Then they turned his flank; an immediate withdrawal was ordered.

At the edge of the village, however, trouble was waiting – and it came in the squat, ugly shape of a Sherman. There it was, rumbling around a bend in the road, spitting flame. Meyer, in his jeep, realised that he would be as trapped as a choice butterfly pinned to a collector's card. The jeep and he would have to part company. As he jumped, Meyer spotted a stone wall with a farmhouse beyond. Pursued by machine fire, he knifed ahead – only to see with a shock that luck had deserted him still further. That particular farmhouse, which had seemed like a safe haven, had a rear dug in solid rock. There was no way out.

At least, Meyer had the consolation of not being alone. Sturmbannfuehrer Max Bornhoeft, a trusted comrade, was by his side. The pair huddled together in a chicken coop, the only possible shelter. The Americans had evidently lost interest and gone away, but there was still the very real threat of the Belgian partisans, called the White Army because of the white overalls which were their uniform. Meyer knew that the end would be extremely painful at the hands of fighters such as these; an SS uniform would be a passport to a slow death.

To be trapped in a chicken coop when it was raining was not the most pleasant of predicaments, but Meyer blessed the sudden change in the weather. The Belgian partisans, after all, were not professional soldiers. As with all amateur fighters, bad weather was likely to drive them indoors.

A move had to be made. Gingerly, the two SS officers left the cover of the chicken coop. Their next refuge was a graveyard, made all the more macabre by the rivulets of rain coursing from the ornate crosses. Any illusion that they would be left alone was swiftly dashed; two policemen were running into the churchyard, weapons drawn. Meyer was on his feet, zigzagging for a wall that was all of fifteen feet. As he landed on the other side, his legs felt as if they had been telescoped up to his neck. Bornhoeft had fared a lot worse; the Sturmbannfuehrer let out a cry of pain and dropped to the ground. Meyer kept on running; this time shelter was a wooden barn.

And that was where 'Panzer' Meyer's war came to an end. There was a shout. A young boy, looking slightly ridiculous with a carbine that was much too big for him, had spotted the fugitive in a barn. The wooden door was shattered by two shots.

Then someone was yelling: '*Come out!*'

Meyer swung his weapon in the direction of the boy and detected fear in the young eyes. He shouted: 'I could shoot your boy, but I won't, if you treat me correctly.'

The father grabbed his son, nodding vigorously at the SS man. Meyer dropped his pistol to the floor. He was in the hands of a Belgian farmer and his fourteen-year-old son.

The survivors had reached the protection of the Sieg-fried Line, the Great Wall of Germany which Hitler had constructed in the 1930s with a massive recruitment of labour from all over the Third Reich. The 12th SS-Panzer Division was virtually non-existent. There was merely a handful of tanks and no cannon to speak of.

It looked as if for the rest of the war Hitler Youth would be fighting with light infantry hand guns. What was more, as well as the Americans, the Canadians and the Belgian partisans, they were facing yet another enemy.

This one was inside the Third Reich itself.

15

For Nazi Germany, the mounting reverses of the battle-field provided gloom enough. The Red Army was moving inexorably towards the borders of the Reich and the Allies slogging through Normandy.

But opposition was running wild on German city streets too, striking at night with such crude acts of sabotage as Molotov cocktails fashioned from the siphoned-off diesel of army trucks or even broken milk bottles placed beneath the wheels of military vehicles.

And there were the slogans scrawled on the walls of public buildings; Gestapo headquarters in a number of cities were disfigured with legends that a few years before would have been unthinkable: 'One people, one nation, one pile of rubble', 'The Allied forces are on the attack on all fronts' and 'Thousands of German soldiers die for the mad cause of Adolf Hitler'.

What was even more inconceivable was that such rebellion came from the young actually *inside* Germany. Those disciples of Schirach and Axmann who remained loyal to National Socialism now found themselves clash-ing with opposition groups whose idealism and patriot-ism were directed, not in support of a Nordic ideal, which was against the Jews and Bolshevism, but against the Nazi state itself.

News of the appalling bloodbath in the ranks of 12th SS-Panzer inevitably reached the homes of stricken families; but disillusion had already bitten deep into those too young to fight.

The youth movement under Hitler had stolen millions of innocent childhoods. Life had become mere para-military drill, with pointless exercises in obedience, frequently supervised by youth leaders scarcely any older than the rank and file. After the war, one soured Hitler Youth member remembered bitterly: ' . . . We were politically programmed to obey orders, to cultivate a soldierly "virtue" of standing to attention and saying "Yes, Sir" and to stop thinking when the magic word "Fatherland" was uttered and Germany's honour and greatness were mentioned.'

With bombs raining down on German cities, some of the most cherished dreams of Hitler Youth withered. Many of the disciples had seen themselves as heroes in the struggle; the war was to put paid to that.

Rebellion had long simmered in Munich. There was an act of spontaneous protest within Hitler Youth during an April 1944 rally. The gathering, in a Munich cinema, was held in the wake of a major air raid, and among those attending were many youths who had come, dirty and dishevelled, from salvage work in the devastated streets.

Their reward was to be upbraided by a Hitler Youth leader on their 'slovenly appearance'. This proved too much for the audience, who hurled abuse; the red-faced leader was forced to leave the platform, lucky to escape with his life.

Nevertheless, since all opposition was spearheaded by children and adolescents, trappings of boy-scout romanticism inevitably stuck.

Notable in the Rhineland area was the organisation known as the Edelweiss Pirates, which had long defied the ban on 'anti-State' organisations. Its members had decked themselves out in checked shirts, colourful neckties and stick-pins with the skull-and-crossbones motif.

It had all seemed so innocent once. Like their fellows in the Hitler Youth, the pirates had relished the weekend camps with their guitar-playing and folk songs. The difference was that they had not enjoyed the protection of the state; their activities were subversive and therefore illegal.

But increasingly the rape of their cities by an enemy that was plainly going to win began to dampen any sense of adventure. It was no longer a game, but deadly reality, with the fear of persecution driving members underground. They met after dark, on street corners and in doorways and cafés. And because they existed only under the shadow of the Gestapo and there was a risk of interrogation, they adopted nicknames such as 'Texas Jack', 'Jonny' and 'Whiskey Bill'.

With increasing exasperation, the various Nazi organisations endured the Pirates' acts of sabotage and subversion. Typical was the complaint from the Duesseldorf-Grafenberg branch of the party:

Re Edelweiss Pirates. The said youth are throwing their weight around again. I have been told that gatherings of young people have become more conspicuous than ever especially since the last raid on Duesseldorf. These adolescents, aged between 12 and 17, hang around into the late evening with musical instruments and young females. Since this riffraff is in large part outside the Hitler Youth and adopts a hostile attitude towards the organisation, they represent a danger to other young people. It has been established recently that members of the armed forces too are to be found among these young people and they, owing to their membership in the Wehrmacht, exhibit particularly arrogant behaviour. There is a suspicion that it is these youths who have covered the walls of the Altenbergstrasse with the slogans 'Down with Hitler', 'The Military High Command is lying', 'Medals for Murder', 'Down with Nazi brutality' etc. However often these inscriptions are removed, within a few days new ones reappear on the walls.

The elimination of anyone caught being a member of illegal cliques such as the Edelweiss Pirates or the White Rose or the Black Gang was one obvious solution. The vast bureaucratic machinery of the Reichssicherheithauptamt – the State Security Office – which included the Gestapo, was retuned to encompass a separate youth department at its notorious Prinz Albrechtstrasse headquarters in Berlin. A 'concentration camp for youth' was opened in the Rhineland town of Neuwied, where boys under twenty years of age were imprisoned.

Yet imprisonment and execution for dissidents was a luxury that Germany, now fighting a war on two fronts and short of cannon fodder, simply could not afford. Although Gestapo arrests were stepped up throughout 1944, youthful offenders soon found they were destined, not for the rope or the guillotine, but for forced labour in the armaments factories or on the sites of shattered railway stations and public buildings.

But at the insistence of Himmler, arrests, interrogations and torture continued, much of it with the enthusiastic cooperation of the HJ Streifendienst, the military police section of Hitler Youth, with particular hatred for the Edelweiss Pirates. Hitler Youth members were encouraged to infiltrate the rebel groups under the guise of sympathisers. Soon the Gestapo cellars were swollen with fresh-faced youngsters, many of whose group activities had been scarcely more sinister than those of the average scout troop.

Most of the suspects were beaten up and released with a warning. A few ended in Dachau concentration camp.

Towards the war's end, the mood changed to full repression. In October 1944, the Gestapo launched a vast sweep on the various illegal underground organisations, including the Edelweiss Pirates. Executions at Cologne-Ehrenfelt, before a crowd of one thousand, were photographed in horrific detail. Adolescents – the youngest was sixteen – struggled slowly on a makeshift gallows.

For the university students of Germany, above all, ten years of Hitler's rule had brought cruel disillusion, sharpened by the defeat at Stalingrad and Germany's failure to win the war. A student revolt in Munich demonstrated these feelings. To Hitler and the veteran Nazis this was a personal insult; their movement, after all, had been born in Bavaria.

One of the leaders of dissent in Munich was a twenty-three-year-old medical student, Hans Scholl, and his sister Sophie, four years younger. All five Scholl children – their father was a mild, liberal Protestant evangelist – had joined the Hitler Youth in 1933. They had embraced the Nazi movement with all the fervour and patriotism of which they were capable. One of the children who survived the war, Inge Scholl, described their feelings in the very early days:

> We loved our homeland, its forests and the River Danube . . . we thought of the smell of heathland, of damp earth and fragrant apples. And Hitler, so we were told everywhere, wanted to give this homeland greatness, happiness and prosperity . . . he wanted to ensure that everyone had work and bread; he would not rest until every German was free and happy in the Fatherland.

Hans was the first to experience flickers of doubt. His local youth leader told him that it was 'wrong' to sing foreign as well as German songs, and he came to object to officious party members 'supervising' his reading, confiscating favourite works by Stefan Zweig and Thomas Mann.

At Munich University, the Scholls, with their movement known as the White Rose (adopted as a symbol of purity), scattered pamphlets openly calling on German youth to rise.

The contents of the pamphlets were too seditious for the Gestapo to ignore:

Appeal to All Germans

The war is approaching its certain end. As in 1918 the German Government tries to direct attention to the growing U-boat danger, while in the East the armies stream backwards incessantly and in the West the invasion is expected. America's armaments production has not yet reached its highpoint, but even today it surpasses everything so far witnessed by history. Hitler leads the German people with mathematical certainty into the abyss. *Hitler can no longer win the war, he can only prolong it!* His guilt and that of his aides has infinitely surpassed any measure. Just punishment comes closer and closer.

But what do the Germans do? They see nothing and hear nothing. They blindly follow their seducers into ruin. Victory at any price is written in its banners. I fight to the last man, says Hitler – while the war is lost already.

Germans! Do you and your children want to suffer the same fate as that suffered by the Jews? Do you want to be measured with the same yardstick as your seducers? Shall we be forever the most hated people in the world? No. Therefore part company with the

137

National Socialist subhumans . . .

Freedom of speech, freedom of religion, protection of the individual citizens from the arbitrary actions of criminal terror-states, these are the foundations for a new Europe. Support the resistance movement and hand on the leaflets.

Less than a fortnight after the fall of Stalingrad, on the morning of 16 February 1943, citizens of Munich on their way to work came face-to-face with 'Freedom' and 'Down With Hitler' daubed on the walls of public buildings. Two days later, Hans and Sophie Scholl were leafleting within the university. They were swiftly denounced, arrested and rushed to Gestapo headquarters.

The result of the trial before the Volksgerichtshof – People's Court – was predictable and swift. The sentence was death by decapitation. Sophie was the first to die, 'free, fearless and with a smile on her face'. In his last moments, Hans Scholl's shout resounded through the bleak corridors of the Munich-Stadelheim prison: 'Long live liberty.'

The White Rose movement was by no means the only group whose members were dispatched by the People's Court. The president of the court was the notorious Roland Freisler, the one-time Communist and ardent disciple of Andrei Vyshinsky who, as chief prosecutor in the Moscow trials of the 1930s, had perfected a brutal technique towards leading generals who had displeased Stalin. Indeed, Hitler had described Freisler as 'our Vyshinsky'.

In the closing months of 1944, something like hysteria gripped sections of Berlin. Spot searches were carried out by the SS and Gestapo; betrayals of alleged traitors were commonplace.

A certain Hitler Youth dissident known simply by the cover name 'Kurt' was an active member of the resistance organisation, Group Y. He had been helping to douse fires after an air raid.

In a moment of ecstatic folly, he predicted: 'Fires like this will consume the Third Reich.'

An eavesdropper denounced him forthwith. The results were arrest and trial before the People's Court. More out of habit than anything else, the Gestapo beat him up before he appeared in the dock.

Another Hitler Youth member of Group Y, known as 'Grete', managed to obtain a pass to the People's Court. Later she described the scene:

I hardly recognised Kurt. They had beaten him mercilessly. To complete his humiliation, they had taken away his braces, his belt and his tie, so that he had to clutch his trousers to prevent them falling down. All this amused the President of the Court, the unspeakable Roland Freisler . . . and the audience; for it was like being at a circus, or seeing, again enacted, the throwing of the Christians to the lions in Ancient Rome. 'It's better than the theatre,' said a woman sitting next to me. There was one brave man sentenced to death before Kurt was brought in. He was accused of distributing subversive leaflets. When Freisler began to amuse the Court at the poor victim's expense, the man in the dock retorted: 'You must hurry up getting me hanged, Herr President, or you will be strung up before me.' Kurt's lawyer was hopeless. He pointed out that Kurt was still a schoolboy, and that he did not mean any harm. Also that his father was a soldier who had been awarded the Iron Cross. This infuriated Freisler all the more. The son should have known better. When sentence of death was pronounced, they dragged Kurt out and his mother collapsed. He saw me and tried to smile.

Kurt was hanged immediately he was taken from

court. The news of the execution was not the only ordeal his parents faced.

The next day they received 'an account' from the SS. It read:

Fee for Death Penalty	Rm 280.30
Fee for Counsel for Defence	Rm 106.50
Charge for Maintenance in Prison	Rm 52.60
Charge for carrying out the sentence	Rm 161.30
Postage	Rm 2.10
	Rm 602.80

The wireless sets belonging to Group Y had their dials always pointing to a Reich station so that the Gestapo could not catch their owners unawares. But the truth could only be gathered by listening to BBC news bulletins, and to do that the members of the group moved from house to house and cellar to cellar. Even to type a leaflet was to run a dangerous risk; typewriters and roneo machines had to be registered so that their owners and buyers were known to the state. The Gestapo, with all their old thoroughness, made regular checks. Even the most perfectly typed leaflets could not conceal peculiarities in letters and typefaces. But Group Y had a stroke of luck, finding an old typewriter that had belonged to an American firm in business before the war in Berlin. Leaflets were thrust into empty soap-powder, tea and soup packets, which were put into the stores. They could scarcely fail to reach the housewives who were suffering, not only from the rationing, but also from the absence of their menfolk at the front.

In January 1945, the BBC broadcast to Europe:

News has reached us of a spirit of revolt against the Nazis among the boys and girls in Germany. The number of these young people, scattered throughout Germany, is evidently large enough to cause Himmler great concern at this critical moment. The German youth below the age of twenty is tired of the regimentation, constraint and propaganda of the National Socialists. They want fresh air, freedom and truth in their lives, and are doing much to awaken the older generations to the reality of the situation by showing them the possibilities of resistance to the Gestapo.

In several cities, these anti-fascist groups of boys and girls feel a close empathy with the foreign workers. Sometimes the members of this youth opposition may be recognised by certain distinguishing features, of which the most commonly seen is the edelweiss worn beneath the facing of their coats. This alpine flower, which blooms high up in the mountains where no other can survive, is adopted by these young Germans as a symbol of the reblossoming of freedom in a land where freedom has been crushed to death . . .

But this was very far from being the story of all the young people in Germany. Fanatical loyalty to Hitler Youth still flourished on the battlefield and, even after the débâcle there, thrived in the bombed, blackened ruins of the capital of the Reich itself.

But the finale in the German capital was not yet to be. For, following the bloody breakout at Caen, Adolf Hitler had embarked on another monstrous gamble in which 12th SS-Panzer had its role.

16

Winter comes early to the remote, semi-mountainous region of the Belgian Ardennes. Rain and snow alternate from mid-November to mid-December, and after that there is no relief from the sleet, snow and cold. It is a depressing place; the trees of the evergreen forest are brushed by clouds in a world of perpetual mists and fog.

Then there is the Eifel, the German extension of the Ardennes, and it was there that the gambler's eye of the supreme warlord alighted. One last tilt at the wheel of fortune! One master-stroke of such audacity that the Allies would gasp and run!

And that was why from the cold stillness there suddenly erupted the rage of battle, a monstrous nightmare of noise from the dull, throaty snarl of guns and the clatter of engines and tracks.

Out of that heavy mist of 16 December 1944, hundreds of tanks and thousands of men emerged for the engagement which war historians call the Battle of the Ardennes, but the Americans have dubbed for all time 'the Battle of the Bulge' – the bulge that the German attack created in the enemy's severely depleted lines.

This was to be no isolated counter-attack by the beleaguered German forces. Generaloberst Hasso-Eccard von Manteuffel, the new commander of 5th Panzer Army, had urged: 'Forward, march, march! In remembrance of our dead comrades, and therefore on their orders, in remembrance of the tradition of our proud Wehrmacht.'

What was afoot?

Hitler's optimism for the success of his latest scheme was rooted in the fortunes of the Allies over the previous months.

Eisenhower's army had become bogged down on the German frontier west of the Rhine by mid-September. There had been triumphs for the Allies, of course. At the end of October, Aachen, north-east of Liège, had surrendered to 1st Army. Eisenhower envisaged a hard slog to the Rhine, but had so far failed to bring it off. His forces, some German generals argued, could be held at bay by a thick wall of defence. But, as past experience had shown, defence was not a concept for which the Nazi warlord cared. His instincts were to break out, to hit the other side a monstrous, stunning blow. Put at its simplest, they would strike through the American line in the Ardennes, then cross the River Meuse and recapture Antwerp.

Hitler's memories turned fondly to 1940. In those days of high euphoria and easy victories, when the original 'Plan Yellow' for the campaign against France had fallen into Allied hands, he had been forced to find a way of regaining the surprise initiative. He had decided then to launch his thrust through the Ardennes, hitherto considered impassable for mechanised armies. The result had been sensational success for the so-called 'Sichelschnitt' – scythe stroke – the drive through the Ardennes and then the right hook. In an almost unbelievable two weeks, the British had been shoved back to the beaches. The Maginot Line had been unhinged. It could all be done again.

Out in front this time, announced Hitler, would be his glorious SS legions. Their formations would be grouped together as 6th Panzer Army, which would give Oberstgruppenfuehrer Sepp Dietrich four Panzer and five infantry divisions.

The American line from Monschau in the north to the Losheim Gap in the south was known to be weakly held.

Once the infantry divisions had secured the initial break-through, then the initiative would pass to the Panzers, in particular the Leibstandarte.

There were numerous flaws to this beautiful dream. For this latest grand design, the Fuehrer could only muster twenty-six divisions, half of his total strength on the western front. The 1,400 tanks and self-propelled assault-guns would go into battle at the expense of the defence in the east, where the Russians pursued relentlessly their roller-coaster advance.

Even a cursory look at the figures would have shown Hitler that he was on a course of disaster. In 1940, the advance to the Channel through the Ardennes had been launched with forty-four divisions, which later rose to seventy-one. There was no possible way in which Hitler could make up the shortfall; it was a monstrous, irresponsible gamble, but the Fuehrer was determined to take it.

What did the reliable Dietrich have to offer?

His army was made up of nine divisions, but hopes were pinned chiefly on two units. There was, of course, Dietrich's own 1st SS-Panzer. And there was the Hitler Youth, now under the command of SS-Standartenfuehrer (later promoted to SS-Oberfuehrer and subsequently to SS-Brigadefuehrer und Generalmajor der Waffen-SS) Hugo Kraas. So that these units could strike out towards the Meuse and thus reach Antwerp, three of Dietrich's infantry divisions were assigned to punch an opening in the American front. The holes would give the Panzers access to two crucial roads, running more or less parallel.

The Hitler Youth would be to the north, with the task of overrunning US positions on the long high rise of the Elsenborn Ridge. At the key village of Malmédy, so went the scheme, 12th SS-Panzer would swing north-west through the town of Spa to the Meuse bridges at Amay and Engis, near Liège.

The 1st SS, under SS-Oberfuehrer Wilhelm Mohnke, would take the southerly route, a network of less-than-perfect roads beginning near Lanzerath and leading to the Meuse bridge at Huy, some fifty miles away.

The generals reacted according to their temperaments. These ranged from horror to indignation to sheer incredulity. In fact, few of them wanted much to do with Hitler's scenario. When, on 24 October, Generalfeldmarschall Rundstedt was presented with the plan, he relates:

> I was staggered . . . It was obvious to me that the available forces were far too small – in fact no soldier really believed that the aim of reaching Antwerp was practicable. But I knew by now that it was impossible to protest to Hitler about the *possibility* of anything.

But Rundstedt did suggest to Hitler that a more modest operation would make better sense. He was brushed aside.

As for Sepp Dietrich, he exploded with barrack-room crudity, but managed to contain himself to the extent of making for the Fuehrer's HQ, grimly waving an all-important 'secret' folder. Demands to see Hitler were coldly refused; Generaloberst Jodl was assigned to deal with him. Both men totally detested one another. As Jodl made to speak, Dietrich cut in: 'I came here to find out if this was some sort of joke. Do you realise what this plan is going to mean to me and my army? I'm expected to get to the Meuse in two days, cross it, capture Brussels and then Antwerp.

'Just like cutting through butter, I suppose. And in the dead of winter. The chances are we'll be up to our neck in snow.'

Jodl, far too spineless ever to have opposed Hitler on anything, merely replied: 'The Fuehrer assures me that the campaign has been well worked out.'

145

It was not just the time-scale that bothered Dietrich. Certainly, there would be twenty-four divisions involved overall; that was an impressive number. But as far as the infantry was concerned, most of the men were undergoing baptism of fire. After the war, Dietrich told Allied inquisitors: 'Just about every unit had been thrashed. There was massive refitting and reforming. As for the calibre of manpower, it was the sweepings. We had utterly unsuited, inadequately trained divisions but the Fuehrer was all for the offensive thrust and there was nothing to be done.'

Hitler was not there in person, but his spirit was. The Fuehrer had planned the route of the SS personally. Dietrich at this point was a mere office-boy conveying instructions; deviation from them in any respect, Hitler had made clear, would be high treason.

Dietrich, conquering his considerable misgivings, prepared to brief the head of his division's Battle Group, upon whom the success of the breakthrough would largely depend.

There was certainly nothing wrong with the man who gave his name to Kampfgruppe – Battle Group – Peiper. Handsome, young, dedicated and loyal, SS-Obersturmbannfuehrer Jochen Peiper, who had once been Adjutant to Reichsfuehrer Himmler, was bold and aggressive in action, a skilled fighting man who spared neither himself nor his men, and certainly never the enemy.

Now Peiper had command of the most important unit in the entire battle-line; his superiors believed he would display all the ruthlessness he had previously shown in Greece and on the Russian front.

His Kampfgruppe, with a strength of around 5,000 men, comprised 1st Panzer Battalion of 22nd SS-Panzer Grenadier Regiment, SS-Reconnaissance Battalion, artillery, anti-aircraft guns and ancillary personnel and material. His task was to keep this force on the move, ignoring all threats to his flanks, across a frighteningly narrow region rich in bends and distinctly dubious as a passage for armoured vehicles.

His route to Antwerp would take him west through the village of Honsfeld and on to Baugnez. After that, it would be south to Ligneuville, with a westward strike to Stavelot on the Ambleve river, arriving finally at Trois Points, the key river crossing in the Ambleve valley. Here a good motor road, excellent for armour, would lead on to Antwerp.

On that dark and bitter D-Day, Saturday 16 December, at 0400 hours, Peiper's tanks rolled. Ahead of the column, the dark winter sky lit up as the artillery erupted in a forty-five-minute drum-fire upon the forward American positions. Behind the initial barrage stormed the assault divisions of 1st SS-Panzer Corps.

The German shock troops, emerging from the thick winter mists, overwhelmed the dazed Americans in the front line. In the American rear area, German infiltrators, dressed in American uniform, cut telephone wires and spread confusion.

Something like blind panic gripped the Americans. At Manderfeld, HQ of 14th US Cavalry Group and now directly in the path of Manteuffel's 5th Panzer Army, staff officers lost their nerve completely. They fled in their vehicles, and in a desperate bid to dispose of anything which might aid the Germans, put the town to the torch.

The opening drive of the Battle of the Bulge shattered two entire American divisions spread along the Schnee Eifel ridge in the north and along the River Our in the south.

It was four days before the Americans pulled themselves together. Dismissals and courts martial abounded.

After that, the American front held. Here, early on in the offensive of the Ardennes, were the youths of 12th

SS-Panzer Division Hitlerjugend, thrust prematurely into action. But their moment of glory did not come yet; the American front was unbreached and a number of strategically important villages were lost.

Kampfgruppe Peiper kept on going, the sheer ruthlessness of the commander's entire approach to warmaking demonstrated graphically when he placed two captured Shermans in the lead to fool the Americans.

His objective was the vital enemy fuel supply dump at the village of Buellingen, north-west of Baugnez.

Buellingen had a special significance for Peiper: it was not on the route laid down for him by Dietrich and therefore by Hitler. Jochen Peiper, hero of the Waffen-SS and darling of Heinrich Himmler, had disobeyed orders deliberately.

The penalty for such insubordination at this stage of the war was death. But Peiper scarcely worried – he had no intention of staying in Buellingen for long.

His advance on the original route, in fact, should have been along a road leading to Schoppen; it turned out to be little more than a long streak of mud and slush. Petrol supplies had been dwindling but, happily, there was an American fuel dump at Buellingen. Peiper turned off. A small garrison of engineers was soon overcome. A dozen American liaison aircraft on the ground were put out of commission and 50,000 gallons of fuel captured.

Peiper had reason to congratulate himself; Standartenfuehrer Kraas had other emotions. For Buellingen was on Rollbahn C, a route assigned to the Hitler Youth. Peiper plainly had not cared a damn about 12th SS-Panzer; his job had been to get his tanks to the Meuse.

Kraas reflected that his division was not getting much of a show. He was soon to think otherwise.

The task of 12th SS-Panzer was now to clear the way through Buellingen and widen the gap in the American lines so that Dietrich could pass through his reserve formations. Indeed, Buellingen was reoccupied briefly by American units after Kampfgruppe Peiper had left. But it was not long in changing hands again.

During the night of 18 December, the first elements of 12th SS-Panzer gathered for the attack against a ridge near Dom Buetgenbach, a cluster of large houses and farm buildings, part of an estate lying out of the village.

Inside Buellingen itself, twenty young Hitler Youth recruits, quartered inside in the house of farmer Albert Kohnenmerger, slept in the cellars. Most were boys, fifteen to seventeen years old. They had already seen action: all knew something of the terrible wrath of the American artillery. Kohnenmerger was with them when the orders came which sent them back to the front. Many, as they gathered their gear to move out into the cold night, wept with fear.

And they had reason.

17

Some three hours before dawn on 21 December, guns, mortars and rockets pounded the foxholes of the Americans, who replied with a frenzy of fire.

Hitler Youth members managed to tear vast gaps in the resistance; even so, only a few Panzers emerged through the storm of exploding shells and out of the cloying mud. The anti-tank guns destroyed, the Panzers drove along the line, raking the foxholes with machine-gun fire and wiping out positions as they went.

There was none of the comfort of infantry support; three Panzer IVs rumbled towards buildings, firing pointblank into houses and barns forming an American

CP. The Americans replied with everything they had; the Panzers remained firm. Eventually two were disabled and the third escaped. The daily situation report of Panzer Corps was terse: *'Angriff 12. SS-Panzer-Division und 12. Volks-Grenadier-Division auf Buetgenbach drang nicht durch.'*

In a nutshell, stalemate.

In the Krinkelt-Rocherath area, to the north-east of Buetgenbach, 12th SS-Panzer had suffered heavy losses. A company commander of the American 23rd Regiment, Captain Charles Macdonald, described the German infantry storming his line. Exchanging volley after volley:

> Germans fell left and right. The few rounds of artillery we did succeed in bringing down caught the attackers in the draw to our front, and we could hear their screams of pain when the small arms fire would slacken.
>
> But still they came!
>
> Seven times they came, and seven times they were greeted by a hail of small arms fire and hand grenades that sent them reeling down the hill, leaving behind a growing pile of dead and wounded.

An account by a German company commander gives a graphic picture of the peculiar cat-and-mouse nature of this war:

> . . . On the right there was a row of tall spruces running parallel with the direction we were taking. These stood on the highest point of the meadow, with a slope leading gently up to them, but with nothing to be seen on the far side. It was in this area of dead ground that the objective of our attack had to be lying. There were still some clouds of mist which had spread over the meadow, but these soon cleared

away. Instinctively, as if in response to an order, all the turrets swung round towards the row of trees on our right flank. There had been no firing yet, but the silence seemed ominous. As we moved on, we sent one or two bursts into the trees with our machine guns, by way of initiating the fight against an imaginary enemy. We sensed however that there was an enemy somewhere out there, excellently camouflaged, and sitting watching us through the eye-pieces of his anti-tank gun sights . . .

SS-Untersturmfuehrer Schittenhelm had just reached the projecting border of the woods when a spout of flame shot out from the rear of his tank, as if it came from a spectral hand. The Panzer was hidden by thick, black smoke mushrooming up – two men managed to get out of it.

Hauptmann Hils gave the order to get ready for action. He was standing in his turret and studying his map to make an exact check on his position. Then he fired a flare to indicate the direction to be taken by the attack. The flare died away over the downward-sloping terrain. Now we waited for the 'Marsch! Marsch!' order to attack. As nothing happened, I took another look at his tank. The turret was burning and there was no sign of Hauptmann Hils any more. The crew were abandoning the tank: I could recognise the driver, SS-Unterscharfuehrer Bunke, and likewise the radio operator, whose name I didn't know. I unfortunately had to accept that the rest of the crew, which as well as Hauptmann Hils included the gunner Lopentzen and the gunlayer Krieg, had become casualties.

There was to be no respite; from the American artillery issued a merciless hail of fire. In no time at all the meadow had become a ploughed-up field and a number of Panzers perished under direct hits. Well-directed bazooka fire poured into Untersturmfuehrer Engel's Panzer, which he had pulled back into the wood for extra protection. From there he had been able to report over the radio, estimating that there were at least two anti-tank guns in the row of spruces which had originally aroused the Germans' suspicion.

Effective direct fire was not possible; instead, a quick succession of high-explosive shells arrowed into the tree-tops. Engel reckoned that the splinters from the shells might put the crews of the American anti-tank guns out of action. To his elation, he saw a number of Americans running away from blazing wrecks towards the shelter of the woods. Now the tank was being swung round towards the row of trees. The terrain was in full view; Engel opened fire.

Any satisfaction was brief. The artillery was starting again with fire ripping into the Panzer. SS-Sturmmann Fitz gained his liberty at the price of a finger. Harassed by the barrage, the crew succeeded in carrying a badly wounded infantryman out of the area of fire.

An American eye-witness described the turmoil in his own lines:

> Aid stations overflowing, wounded men being evacu-ated by Jeep, truck, ambulance, anything that could roll, walking wounded, prisoners going back under guard, trucks rolling up to the front with ammunition and supplies and firing at the same time at low-flying airplanes. Vehicles off the road, mired in mud or slush or damaged by gunfire only to be manhandled off the traffic lane to open the road: signal men trying to string wire to elements to cut off or to repair lines which were being shot out as fast as they were put in.

Dom Buetgenbach had not been taken that day, but there was to be only a few more hours' grace before the next attempt. At 0630 hours on 22 December, Kampfgruppe Kuhlmann tried again, this time further west. But it was merely a series of inconclusive engagements with the much depleted ranks of Grenadiers pulling back, with several Panzers left behind.

Artillery support was a commodity fatally denied to the SS Panzers. And what infantry there was had too few assault guns; in any case, the Americans had the major advantage in numbers. The offensive in the northern sector ground to a halt.

But it was by no means in the nature of the SS to give up just yet. The German maintenance units struggled manfully to recover what Panzers they could. Willi Fischer, whose Panzer had been disabled at Krinkelt, to the north-east of Dom Buetgenbach, attempted to make the best of the most unseasonable Christmas he had ever spent:

. . . We were able to clean up a completely abandoned food depot, after which the company later enjoyed many goodies. We had become self-sufficient. Over the Christmas period we moved into rooms in a peasant's house as the cold in the Panzer had become unbearable. Our rest period during those days was marred by constant mortar-fire. With great difficulty, and after all the efforts of two 18-ton tractors had failed, we were towed into the workshops by an armoured recovery vehicle.

Another Panzer commander, Heinze Linke, whose Panzer had lost a track on a mine during the attack on Dom Buetgenbach, had to take shelter time and again while his tank was being coupled to its recovery vehicle. But it stuck obstinately in the frozen mud, and when it was eventually released the agony was still only just beginning. American fire-power at its most vicious was concentrated outside Buellingen. Linke related: ' . . . The recovery vehicle burst into flames and it wasn't long before we caught it too. All of us except SS-Untersturm-fuehrer Jansen were out in the open. He got a splinter in his backside but could still walk. In no time at all both Panzers were blazing.'

All attempts to dislodge the Americans from Elsenborn Ridge had failed. Even Peiper had failed. By Saturday, 23 December, his Tigers were dug in hopelessly at the key village of La Gleize, which the Americans had ringed in anticipation of an attack by fighter bombers.

In Malmédy, safe in American hands, troops and inhabitants glimpsed the American bombers in the bright sunlight. And then everyone was diving frantically for shelter as the bombs rained down. It was an exercise in total destruction. The old pre-war Malmédy ceased to exist, and the wounded lay groaning beneath mountains of rubble. There was no water pressure for the fire hoses; the centre of Malmédy blazed and engineers had to use explosives to keep the fire within check.

Most of Battle Group Peiper was forced into the cellars of La Gleize; the SS refused even now to admit defeat. Every time American tanks and infantry tried to follow up the bombardment they came up against a solid wall of dug-in Panzers and anti-tank guns.

It was not war, but slaughter. Even Peiper could not be blind to the figures: 800 left of 5,000 who had gone in just a week before. On Christmas Eve, he was forced to pull out and the Americans of 30th Infantry Division who eventually penetrated La Gleize found smouldering tanks and shattered half-tracks among the rubble.

Eventually, Peiper and his miserable, frozen survivors reached their own lands, the sad ghost of an élite.

Defeat stared Germany in the face; the farce of the Ardennes adventure had surely proved that. But Hitler would concede nothing; the Leibstandarte and Hitler Youth were to work together yet again.

18

What was it Gerd von Rundstedt had said back in October, a bare two months before the battle in the Ardennes?

The Commander-in-Chief West had trumpeted: 'You have brought the enemy to a halt at the gates of the Reich. But he will shortly go over to new super attacks. I expect you to defend Germany's sacred soil with all your strength and to the very last . . . Soldiers of the western front! Every attempt of the enemy to break into our Fatherland will fail because of your unshakeable bearing. Heil the Fuehrer!'

And the truth? The truth had been written high in the blood and slaughter of the month-long battle. The Wehrmacht had suffered an estimated 120,000 casualties. The Luftwaffe had been virtually wiped out.

And what had there been to show for it? About 15,000 casualties had been inflicted on the Allies in the Ardennes, with the result that Allied operations in the Ruhr and the Saar had been postponed for at most six weeks.

It was true that in the field Germany could still call on some five million troops, but the most precious resource of all was dwindling rapidly. In 1944, 106 divisions were destroyed, three more than had been mobilised at the outbreak of war. Hitler still nourished the illusion that there was a large-scale war to be fought, just as there had been in 1939. Each division that perished was replaced with a new one, rather than used to bolster existing units.

Hitler's energetic Armaments Minister, Albert Speer, observed gloomily: 'New divisions were formed in great numbers, equipped with new weapons and sent to the front without any experience or training, while at the same time the good, battle-hardened units bled to death because they were given no replacement weapons or personnel.'

The constant drain on manpower called for desperate measures. Those members of Hitler Youth who had stayed at home and somehow avoided service with 12th SS-Panzer were automatically conscripted at sixteen. Under the direction of Heinrich Himmler, now Commander-in-Chief of the Reserve Army and child-ishly pleased to be 'a real soldier', the youths were mustered for what were referred to pretentiously as Volksgrenadier divisions. They rubbed shoulders with the replacement units, remnants of shattered divisions and depot staffs. They were of little military value, even as defenders; only the fire of their fanaticism kept the illusion burning.

And Hitler had need of such faith; it was flickering ominously on the battlefield.

A deep disillusion now beat hard into the average soldier in the west. The generals had made a new set of promises and held out the prospect of fresh miracles. Instead, there was the relentless catalogue of defeats. Only the Hitler Youth at the front seemed to remain steadfast.

Generalfeldmarschall Rundstedt, sacked twice by Hitler and then reinstated, had served the German Army without complaint or question for thirty-five years. His army group had destroyed Poland and per-formed with conspicuous brilliance in France. Alle-giance to Hitler had stretched back even further than that: he was among those who had approved the liquid-ation of his Fuehrer's rivals in the early brawling, brown-shirt days of power.

156

All that was in the past now; he was sixty-nine and too old to face anything but reality. Compensation could be found in memories and in brandy – the latter in ever-increasing quantities.

There had been one occasion when he and Dietrich and 'Panzer' Meyer had sat under a big oak tree in France and discussed the gloomy situation. Rundstedt had congratulated Meyer on the performance of his teenagers, breathing brandy fumes and croaking: 'But it's a shame that the youth of this country has to be sacrificed in this senseless way.'

It was a view he still held, but the truth was that a good many of the Hitler Youth still seemed willing enough to make that sacrifice for their Fuehrer. Now 12th SS-Panzer survivors, taut, pale and old before their time, were thrust into the hell of battle wherever the going was hardest. And, increasingly for Germany, that was everywhere and anywhere.

As seven Allied armies spread over the Reich, advances exceeded even those of the great pursuit across France. Drives were frequently at the rate of thirty-five to fifty miles a day.

On 1 April 1945 at 1300 hours, the US 1st and 9th Armies sealed off the Ruhr. Then came the order: General Omar Bradley's Twelve Army Group was 'to mop up . . . the Ruhr . . . launch a thrust with its main axis: Kassel-Leipzig . . . seize any opportunity to capture a bridgehead over the River Elbe.'

In pursuit of these orders, both the 9th and the 1st prepared to push forward on a two-corps front. Ninth advanced with one corps on each side of the autobahn penetrating the vast woodland sprawl of the Teuto-burger Wald, near the large industrial town of Bielefeld, crossing the River Weser, the last water barrier before the Elbe.

The newly appointed Generalleutnant Karl Becher, commander of the German front, had a daunting task.

He reflected wryly that in happier times he would have called on some 100,000 men to make up eight or nine divisions. The strength now was a mere 7,000. Furthermore, it was made up of a ragbag. Here were training companies, lower-grade soldiers and even two 'ear battalions', men suffering from ear complaints. Otherwise, there were Volkssturm units – Home Guard – and men from the SS training division stationed at the nearby infantry school at Senne.

The SS men were the only ones worth a light. They might be inexperienced but they were prepared to stand and fight, while the rest panicked. Possibly they could not be blamed; an American tank rumbling towards a position was a daunting sight, particularly when the only opposition available was the cheap, easily manufactured suicide weapon, the Panzerfaust.

Becher took the full power of the American assault on the night of 2/3 April. First, the bombers went in. Then the 9th attacked along the whole 12th and 14th Corps area. Resistance to the north of the autobahn was reasonably light. Most of the task facing Colonel Gilbert Farrand, Chief of Staff of the 5th Armoured Division, was to mock up rearguard actions. There was precious little of war in the classic sense; operations were conducted mainly on guerrilla lines rather than from any firm front.

But that was by no means to underestimate the ferocity of the Germans. That was considerable indeed. The technique was to allow the American armour to penetrate the front, then wait for the infantry to approach, inching its way cautiously through the wooded heights of the Teutoburger Wald. Then the attack would come from the most fanatical members of Hitler Youth, firing indiscriminately into knots of infantry. In the end, of course, they were trapped; but even then they kept on fighting, clinging to their positions to the last man.

Cynical, battle-hardened and merciless towards the SS though they were, the GIs were appalled to find that in many cases their buddies were being shot down by mere children.

Lieutenant-Colonel Roland Kolb of 84th Division noted in one case that his men were up against an 'artillery unit', manned by boys of twelve and under who 'rather than surrender fought until killed'.

The Americans mowed them down.

Resistance proved a lot stiffer south of the autobahn; US Corps was in the thick of it between the town of Detmold and Bielefeld itself. And members of Hitler Youth were dug in south of Detmold; many of them not part of 12th SS-Panzer, but mustered into battle after the barest of military training. Yet they fought as desperately as the older veterans for every inch of ground, and their losses were as heavy. They lacked heavy weapons; their only ally was the thick wood around them, favouring the defender.

Even with the total failure of the offensive in the Ardennes and the virtual collapse of his western front, the Fuehrer did not hesitate to sacrifice still more of the Hitler Youth on the altar of his obsessions.

No matter that his empire had contracted to a narrow corridor in the heart of Germany little more than one hundred miles wide. Now it was the turn of Hungary; what was to be the last German offensive of the war, Operation Fruehlingsverwachen – Spring Awakening – was launched in western Hungary early in March. Budapest was the obsession now; armies (*what* armies?) must be sent to relieve it. Germany must, above all, retain the oil fields of Lake Balaton. Hitler ordered General Otto Wohler's Army Group South to strike towards Budapest and Baja, holding a line across the Danube. The task of 2nd Panzer Army would be to drive south of the lake and head directly east towards the Danube. Sixth Panzer

Army was put in the vanguard of the attack. The spirit of the men soared: their unfortunate showing in the Ardennes would be reversed. Now they had the PzKpfw VI Tiger II – the so-called 'King Tiger' – massively armoured and mounting an 88-mm gun. It was to prove the last fling of Hitler's Panzer armies.

Spring Awakening was undertaken in the most unspeakable conditions. Heavy snow in late February was followed by a sudden rise in temperature at the turn of the month; the roads heaved as they thawed. This capricious turn in the weather had an effect even on the infantry. As for the tanks, they could not move under the cover of night. When they tried they became stuck and could not be released until morning light. By early in March, there were blizzard conditions; many of the tanks could not move at all.

Sepp Dietrich, with his 6th Panzer Army, had rumbled towards Budapest across a devastated Europe with train-load upon train-load of troops.

Constant fuel shortages and bad connections made progress lamentably slow. But the morale of the youths of 12th SS-Panzer Division Hitlerjugend and the rest of Dietrich's army was high indeed. Here was an entirely new theatre of battle with clear cut objectives.

In Budapest, between Lake Balaton and Lake Valence, would come the main thrust; the first objective of the Leibstandarte and 12th SS-Panzer was to force bridgeheads across the Sio canal.

Army Group South lay in a vast arc west of the Danube. Its boundaries extended from the River Drau to the western edge of Lake Balaton. Then the line swung westwards to the Vertes mountains and to the bridgehead established by the Russians on the northern bank of the Danube at Gran. A daring lightning assault secured the bridgehead; a Knight's Cross was the prize for a Panzer commander who wiped out eleven Russian tanks. But the cost had been grim losses; more than

1,000 Grenadiers had been sacrificed by each of the SS divisions and the battle had hardly begun.

On D-Day for Operation Spring Awakening, 6 March 1945, army units raced in a fast motor-boat assault across the Drau; the defence of the Bulgarian Division was effectively shattered. Then from Panzer Army came the main thrust between the lakes; 12th SS-Panzer and the Leibstandarte divisions forced the canal bridgeheads.

But the conditions were unspeakable. The first shock came with the order to start the engines of the Panzers.

Water had seeped into the fuel tanks. With shells flying back and forth, the mechanics got down to the frustrating, time-wasting task of draining out the contaminated fuel, while the search went on for fresh supplies. It was midday before the Leibstandarte was able, once again, to roar into life.

Any dreams the Hitler Youth may have had of snatching glory were doomed. At the very first objective, the division ran into trouble. There was fierce fighting at the village of Oedin-Puszta. The Russian line of defence proved rock solid. The youth of 26th Panzer Grenadier Regiment was sliced into oblivion by the Russian guns. True, there was the isolated success of securing the village of Igar, but that operation and the warding off of Russian counter-attacks took a whole day. And all the time the Panzer Army was bleeding to death; the total strength in tanks and self-propelled guns had dwindled to less than 200 vehicles.

The withdrawal of the Panzer Army to the River Raab in the west could be delayed no longer.

Even that exercise was a heart-breaking, perilous affair; scores of vehicles were bogged down in mud and much heavy equipment had to be abandoned or destroyed.

Mud is no respecter of nationality; even the Russians found their progress slowed. General (later Marshal) Tolbukhin, the fifty-year-old Soviet commander, was eager for new laurels. His 57th Army had played a key role in the encirclement of the Germans at Stalingrad the year before; Stalin still expected much of him. The slowness of the advance threw Tolbukhin into a rage. The order went out to 6th Guard Tanks Army; the pace must be forced regardless of the rate of loss. The troops obeyed, and lost 267 tanks in ten days. But the result was achieved. The thrust carried the Russians across the Austrian frontier.

For the Hitler Youth, the battlefield war was as good as over. But the fighting was to go on – this time, for the defence of the capital of the Reich itself.

19

The Berlin to which Adolf Hitler returned in the last January of the war lay at the mercy of American bombers by day and British by night.

To many observers, fresh destruction from the clouds only seemed to add to the miseries of a city already destroyed; each morning, Berliners gazed at a moonscape of craters and rubble. The dust which hung above the city following each raid drifted down to form a slimy sediment over shattered streets and buildings.

Yet even in April normality was preserved to an astonishing degree; Berliners had an equivalent attitude to the Londoner's 'business as usual'. Somehow, 12,000 policemen had managed to stay at their posts, and the mail continued to be delivered almost until the end. It was still possible to make telephone calls and to use the underground and overhead railways.

Even so, here was a city whose heart had been

wrenched out by the cruelties of war; evacuation, casualties and the call-up of men and women had cut the population by around a third. Most of the males remaining were either under sixteen or over sixty. In the streets, foreign forced labour was still at work; Polish Jews at Koenigswusterhausen toiled away at constructing giant tank-traps.

None of this was seen by Adolf Hitler. Indeed, few Germans knew that their Fuehrer was even in Berlin. He had taken up residence in the new Reich Chancellery, which ironically had been intended as the showpiece of the rebuilt city. Here he lurked behind the strengthened windowpanes, which were hidden by thick grey curtains.

As for the building itself, it had been pounded and pockmarked by bomb blasts, but at least a section of it was habitable. The same could not be said for the houses of those made homeless by the bombing; one in three houses had been destroyed or rendered uninhabitable. In the autumn of 1944 with the strategic air strike reaching its climax, RAF Bomber Command alone had dropped more bombs on Germany than it had during the entire course of the previous year.

It is unlikely that Hitler knew any of this. He rarely ventured outside the Chancellery, sensing treachery in the air ever since he had screamed at Sepp Dietrich and his Waffen-SS for losing in Hungary. Now the SS guards were extra eyes and ears for the Fuehrer; they were seldom allowed to leave his side.

No matter that citizens in towns and cities throughout western Germany were even then greeting British and American troops with displays of bed linen doing duty as the white flags of surrender. No matter that the Americans and Russians were driving swiftly to a junction at the Elbe. The British were at the gates of Hamburg and Bremen; Germany faced expulsion from occupied Denmark. In Italy, Bologna had fallen and the Allied forces poured into the valley of the Po. Vienna had fallen to the Russians on 13 April. Even now they were heading up the Danube. Linz, Hitler's Austrian home town, would see the meeting of the Soviets and the US Third Army. Nuremberg, which Hitler had one day dreamed of making the capital of the Reich, was in a state of siege; Munich could not last long. Hitler would go on living out his fantasies to the end. The world outside was collapsing; very well, he would create one of his own, even if it meant bringing the real one down in a holocaust of blood.

Unlike his fellow citizens, Hitler had an elaborate bolt-hole. He could descend from the new Reich Chancellery to the safest bunker in Berlin, the existence of which was known to few Berliners. Its only outward trace was a square blockhouse and a round pillbox intended as an emergency exit. His cocoon of safety was a rambling catacomb fifty-five feet below ground level, with exterior walls six feet thick, and a roof covered with tons of earth to a depth of thirty feet.

Once, an elaborate, web-like electronic network of communications had sprung across the vassal states of Europe. Now there was just a single switchboard of a type more suited to a provincial hotel than a head of state, one radio, and one radio-telephone to the German High Command at Zossen, south of Berlin. To this Third Reich in miniature Hitler repaired when it became apparent that there was to be no let-up in Allied saturation bombing.

Anyone who can imagine life spent in the crypt of a church will gain some idea of existence in this subterranean cavern of thirty-odd cramped rooms decked out in battleship grey. In places, cement dripped moisture; there had been no time for the builders to complete their work. Just three rooms, ten by fifteen feet – only slightly larger than the rest – plus a toilet and shower, made up the Fuehrer's private quarters.

And Hitler himself?

164

The spindly fingers of death beckoned to this dreadful physical spectre, awash with drugs, hunched and shaking, with faltering voice and staring eyes, his uniform hanging loose, the jacket blotched with fragments of food from hastily snatched meals. The appearance of premature senility was heightened by the slightly wobbling head, the left arm hanging slackly and the hand constantly trembling.

His eyes sometimes blazed with their old fire but usually only when talking of past triumphs. He did not wish to be confronted with inconvenient or disagreeable facts. When, on 9 January, Generaloberst Heinz Guderian had warned: 'The eastern front is like a house of cards', Hitler refused to take it in. Guderian had told him of the enemy forces deployed on the Vistula. Hitler insisted that they were 'the greatest bluff since Genghis Khan'. Three days later the Fuehrer's Vistula front had been ripped to pieces. On 31 January, the Russians had reached the Oder. Marshal Georgi Zhukov drove a salient into east Germany and submitted plans to the Stavka – Soviet High Command – for an all-out assault on Berlin.

And when the time came, who was to defend die Reichshauptstadt – the Reich capital – the shattered hub of the Fuehrer's now microscopic empire?

Certainly not the frail, collapsing military front whose last two intact Panzer armies had been routed by the Americans. There was no longer any élite fighting force, either on the ground or in the air. Reichsmarschall Hermann Goering, the obese drug-ridden head of the Luftwaffe, skulked in his vast country palace, Carinhall, in the Schorfheide, consoled by his looted art treasures and, protected by a personal bodyguard, dreaming of the succession he considered his right.

Little consideration, in fact, had been given to safeguarding Berlin, soon squeezed to an east-west belt ten miles long and three miles wide. Hitler referred grandiosely to 'Fortress Berlin', which scarcely existed. In mid-April, the fortifications expert, General Max Pemsel, took one look at the city's defences and dismissed them as 'utterly futile, ridiculous'.

The city's commandant, Generalleutnant Hellmuth Reymann, belatedly set to work. Defence maps were prepared hastily; slit trenches and isolated pillboxes were marked as major strongpoints. In the centre of the city was the last-ditch defence ring – codenamed Zitadelle – containing command sectors of vast flak towers, massive concrete pyramidal structures impervious to bombs and artillery.

The deficiencies were colossal; it would have been unfair to blame the luckless Reymann for them. Berlin's railway system, for example, which sprouted cuttings, culverts, sidings and overhead railways, would have provided excellent man-made obstacles and anti-tank barriers – if there had been enough troops to man them. Reymann had estimated that he would need at least 200,000 fully trained and equipped troops to defend all of Berlin's 321 square miles.

What he had was 60,000 Volkssturm and Hitler Youth amateurs, who jostled shoulders with engineers, policemen and anti-aircraft crew. Reymann later recounted: 'Their weapons came from every country that Germany had fought with or against. Besides our own issues there were Italian, Russian, French, Czech, Belgian, Dutch and Norwegian guns.' This meagre armoury led to some bizarre cannibalising. Greek bullets were remachined to fit Italian rifles.

Nevertheless, the best possible face had to be put on things. Reymann signed the 'Basic Order for the Preparations to Defend the Capital'. The signature was the General's; the voice belonged unmistakably to Adolf Hitler. The capital must be defended 'to the last man and the last shot'. Furthermore, fighting must be with 'fanaticism, imagination, every means of deception, cunning and deceit; and with improvisations of all kinds – on or above or under the ground'. That each defender was trained in the finer points of the use of weapons was secondary to the need for each to be 'filled with a fanatical desire to fight, that he knows the world is holding its breath as it watches this battle and that the battle for Berlin can decide the war'.

Until the last moment, the youth of Germany was exhorted to mount and assist in the defence of the Reich. Failure to do so meant instant execution by drumhead courts martial designated 'Flying Special Tribunal', set up personally by Hitler. Already eight German officers who commanded the weak forces above the town of Remagen, twenty-five miles down the Rhine from Koblenz, had been summarily executed for failing to hold the river's bridges.

Nobody was exempt. Flying SS court martial squads carried out various dragnets on Berlin's shattered streets. The bodies of 'traitors' swung from lamp posts and trees. Many were Hitler Youth teenagers who had been hauled out of their homes after they fled there in terror or to show off their uniforms.

Their fate was identical; they were dragged away screaming and strung up. Placards pinned to their uniforms read: 'I hang here because I left my unit without permission.'

But there remained the fanatics among 'the young tigers'. Admittedly, their resolution to stand fast had been fuelled by the dire warnings of rape, pillage and destruction that Goebbels had spread about the 'Bolshevik hordes' and 'the Anglo-American gangsters'.

But there was more to it than that. Many in the Hitler Youth felt their hour had come; no longer could they be thrust aside by their prejudiced parents and stupidly arrogant elder brothers. They shovelled away day and night on the earthworks and tank-traps. They looked after refugees and helped the wounded during air raids.

And it was not just the air raids. At 5 a.m. on Monday, 16 April, three red flares soared into the sky above the Kuestrin bridgehead, to the east of Berlin and north-east of Frankfurt. Moments later, 20,000 artillery pieces erupted in a furious bombardment which engulfed the German front line. Forests were set ablaze; a hot, debris-laden wind cascaded back towards Berlin. Some 150 searchlights threw the battlefield into sharp relief, their beams slicing through the dense smoke and dust-clouds.

Zhukov's offensive had begun.

If there was terror on the battlefield, it was nothing, absolutely nothing, compared to what lay in store for Berlin. At 11.30 a.m. on Saturday, 21 April, its people found out.

At first, it sounded like the giant wail of a stricken animal whose sufferings were so unspeakable that not even eventual screaming brought relief. Shoppers at Karstadt's department store on Hermannplatz were puzzled by the sound which seemed at first to be a comfortable distance away. Then, as if some invisible hand had turned up the volume of sound, artillery shells screeched through the streets, hacking anything in their path.

Above all, they hacked through the shoppers. This was not death with a single bullet in one area of the anatomy; this was the ripping apart of bodies, the splashing of portions of flesh against boarded-up shop-fronts.

Out of the heavens hell had come to Berlin. The flames, their greed unsatisfied with tall buildings, rampaged from the rooftops and began to lick the centre of the city. In the Kurfuerstendamm people ran helter-skelter they knew not where, dropping briefcases and packages. One of the most bizarre incidents followed a direct hit on a stable of riding horses at the Tiergarten. The screams of terrified animals mingled with the cries of men and women; then the horses stampeded out of the inferno and straight down the Kurfuerstendamm, manes and tails ablaze.

Against all this was bicycle-borne Hitler Youth, the Panzerfaust strapped to the handlebars. To these almost grotesquely comic formations, Hitler ascribed the grandiose title of a 'tank-destroyer division'. This weird force had been formed in the snow and sleet of midwinter 1945 to take on the Red Army's T-34s.

The 'tank-destroyer division' was at least a shade less fantastic than another of the Fuehrer's schemes in the last months of the war. The forces of Hitler Youth on the ground would be complemented in the air by the Volksjaeger – People's Hunters – which would drive back the enemy from the borders of the Reich. Furthermore, the fighters, to be of light metal and plywood, would be flown by Hitler Youth boys. Two thousand of these jet-powered Heinkel 162s, Hitler demanded, must be in production by 1945. The young pilots would be trained initially on gliders. It was cloud-cuckoo land, the demented dreams of a madman now skulking in his bunker with dark dreams.

In the bunker, hopes were pinned on the 12th Army of General der Panzertruppen Walter Wenck, in the west of Berlin. In the early hours of 23 April, Generalfeldmarschall Keitel arrived at Wenck's headquarters. He snapped: 'The Fuehrer's orders are precise. The battle for Berlin has begun. You will turn east and drive through Potsdam to Berlin.' Wenck had already made his own plans; 12th Army would shift towards Berlin but without relinquishing its position on the Elbe. Thus a corridor would be kept open to the west. Over half a million refugees already surrounded Wenck's army; to save the life of Hitler no longer seemed to have much point. Hitler, crouched in the bunker, was to ask time and time again: *'Wo ist Wenck?'*

Few dared tell him that Wenck was directing German

soldiers and civilians across the Elbe so that they would fall into American rather than Russian hands.

Nobody in Berlin would have thought that the situation could become much worse. It could and did. The Russians had swarmed into food warehouses in the suburbs; in the city stocks were down to two or three days.

'*Wo ist Wenck?*'

Wenck was not there to save his Fuehrer. That job Axmann had now delegated to Hitler Youth.

20

Upon Axmann's personal orders, battalions of Hitler Youth were mustered for the hopeless task of fending off the enemy on the Pichelsdorf Bridge across the River Havel in Berlin. The myth was that Wenck, like the United States cavalry in a western movie, would ride to the rescue of them all.

During his interrogation at the Nuremberg Trials, Axmann countered the charge of sending a battalion of about six hundred boys of fifteen and sixteen to defend the bridge by saying: 'I shall never cease to regret the losses which were suffered then by my young comrades.'

There was much to regret. The dark, menacing outlines of the Russian tanks could be glimpsed in the early dawn, their guns directed towards the bridge. The Hitler Youth troops, either in pairs or alone, crouched with rifles and their Panzerfausts. Only one possible fate awaited them; the Russian artillery barrage was a massacre.

One Hitler Youth survivor related:

Our leader Hauptsbannfuehrer Frischefsky and the police fetched us from our homes and we had to assemble in the SS barracks and on the Schlossplatz. There we were divided into our squads and were attached to the SS and the Volkssturm. We first saw action in the north and east of the city. Most of us were killed by infantry fire because we had to attack across the open fields. Then the fighting in the city. Two days of it. In two days and two nights Oranienburg changed hands four times. That finished another part of us. Then the Russians started bombarding the city . . . and when we wanted to finish and go home we were stopped and had to join the escape across the canal . . . My Jungzugfuehrer who refused was strung up on the nearest tree by a few SS men and an SA man. But then he was already fifteen years old . . . This morning we have been collected again for our next action.

General Karl Weidling might have been forgiven for thinking that he was the unluckiest senior soldier in Berlin. Misfortunes had crowded in. His 56th Panzer Corps had already taken the full brunt of General Georgi Zhukov's onslaught. The corps had managed to keep Zhukov at bay for a full forty-eight hours and Russian casualties had been high. Reserves, however, had been promised. Weidling would have welcomed the presence of the SS Nordland Division and the powerful 18th Panzer Grenadier Division which by some miracle had managed to remain more or less intact.

The absence of SS-Norland Division was, to Weidling's fury, the responsibility of the division's arrogant SS-Brigadefuehrer Joachim Ziegler, who made it very clear that he did not regard 56th Panzer Corps as of high priority. As for the Panzer Grenadiers, they were a whole day late. Weidling commented sarcastically: 'SS-

Nordland Division was at least bang on time – to begin a retreat.'

There had been additional misfortune. Goering's much vaunted 9th Parachute Division proved useless, its personnel fleeing in terror from the Russian guns.

The front of 56th Corps could not hold. The Russians forced the Germans back by applying a cunning horseshoe manoeuvre – hitting from both sides and encircling time and again. Weidling was forced to evacuate two headquarters in one afternoon.

The day was lost. Or was it? Arthur Axmann thought not.

Weidling had taken refuge in a cellar. Axmann burst in enthusiastically: 'My Hitler Youth is willing to fight. My troops are manning the roads in the rear of 56th Corps.'

It was too much for Weidling. He was a ruthless professional soldier, but no butcher. Barely managing to contain his rage, he spluttered at Axmann: 'I refuse to have children sacrificed in a hopeless cause. You will cancel your orders instantly.'

Whitefaced, Axmann withdrew. Whether or not he actually issued the cancellation is not known. What is certain is that it never reached the Hitler Youth. True to their original order, the youngsters held their position. The Russians mowed them all down. Some hours later, they were found heaped in piles, their puny weapons beside them. There were just two survivors, both of whom had fallen asleep during a lull in the battle.

The record of other Hitler Youth members was less creditable. Berlin was in its death throes. All transport within the city ground to a halt; the refrigeration plants ceased to function. At first, shopkeepers did what they could to stop the plundering. Eventually, most gave up in despair, handing supplies to looters rather than risk their premises being torn apart. Klaus Kuester of the

Hitler Youth walked into one shop, brandishing a revolver and demanding food. An aunt who was with him protested: 'You are behaving like an American gangster.' Karl shrugged: 'What does it matter? It's a matter of life and death.'

When a report came that Russian tanks were breaking through from the north-west, sixteen-year-old Lothar Loewe set off with a companion on a reconnaissance of the Sophie-Charlotten-Strasse. Each had been able to muster a bazooka, but Lothar felt decidedly ill at ease with his Italian machine pistol; its defective safety-catch caused it to fire unexpectedly.

They took cover in the cellar of an apartment building. Three tanks approached; Lothar went to work with the bazooka while his comrade covered him with fire from the unpredictable machine pistol.

Lothar's first shell exploded beneath the tracks of the tank, knocking it out. The other two tanks rumbled towards the cellar. The boys fled and were lucky enough not to fall victim to the SS killer squads, but to be given the Iron Cross, Second Class.

However, the day's work was far from over. After a short rest, the two set out to inspect a defence position at the Charlottenburg station. They found themselves in the ground-floor restaurant, where an SS-Unterscharfuehrer was guzzling beer.

The man was a realist. He looked up and grinned: 'Hello, boys. Come and join me.'

And there they sat, Lothar downing schnapps while the others gulped beer and the Russian tanks edged ever nearer.

They found some biscuits and some red wine. Then they filled their pockets with tins of jam and beef and bottles of cognac. After that, they fled.

At around 1520 hours on Monday, 30 April 1945, ten days after his fifty-sixth birthday and twelve years and three months to a day after he became Chancellor of Germany and launched the Third Reich, Adolf Hitler shot himself with his Walther 7.65-calibre pistol, which he had carried in his jacket for several weeks. It is likely that at the same time he bit down on a poison capsule. His wife, Eva Braun, the long-time mistress whom Hitler had married in the small hours of the day before, took poison. The atmosphere of almost surrealist lunacy in the bunker persisted until the end. At lunch time, Hitler had regaled his listeners about the proper breeding of dogs and put forward the theory that grease collected in the Paris sewers was an ingredient of French lipstick.

On the occasion of Hitler's birthday, the Nazi paladins – Speer, Goebbels, Goering, Ribbentrop and the sinister, rasping Fuehrer aide Martin Bormann – had turned up for an uneasy reception. That stilted occasion had been preceded by an interlude that could only be described as bizarre – except that everything in that subterranean world had a hint of madness, rather as if a Marx Brothers movie had been scripted by Salvador Dali.

Berlin was a charnel-house and a ruin. Yet, above ground, in the new Chancellery building, a Hitler Youth delegation waited in wide-eyed astonishment for an audience with its Fuehrer. Even though many of the rooms were little more than shells, it had been possible, somehow, to maintain the vast diplomatic hall. Here, the boys of between twelve and sixteen sat awkwardly on the edge of the chairs while they were served hot chocolate by footmen in dazzling livery. For all the world, it might have been a pre-war soirée.

Once that particular stage setting had served its purpose, Axmann bustled in and herded the youths into the garden of the Chancellery. The door of the bunker opened; Adolf Hitler walked slowly towards his guests, his gait shambling, his eyes tired and glassy. He managed to summon a ghastly jauntiness, issuing decorations to frightened small boys who still saw themselves as street heroes. An aide was left with the job of pinning on the medals. Then Hitler gave a languid wave of his hand and returned to the bunker.

Some loyal associates remained a little longer, then they too left.

Arthur Axmann, among a group of ten eventual escapees, edged his way along the tracks and tunnels of the Friedrichstrasse station, eventually tearing the insignia off his uniform and throwing away his weapons. Emerging into the street, he ran slap into a Russian outpost. Axmann, an experienced campaigner – he had lost an arm fighting in Russia – held on to his nerve.

The Russians took the stragglers for Volkssturm and were prepared to be amiable. They all chatted together for a while, fellow sufferers in what they all agreed was a pointless war. There was even sympathy for Axmann's one arm and a halting attempt at German: 'Voyna [the war] kaputt, Hitler kaputt.'

The Nazis moved on. At dawn, they had reached a bridge at Invalidenstrasse. Heavy tanks were rattling ahead and there was general confusion. Axmann and a companion, Guenther Weltzin, noticed two bodies. One was Martin Bormann and the other Ludwig Stumpfegger, who had been a doctor on Himmler's staff. Apparently, both were dead; there was no sign of blood or injury. Axmann knew that many of the senior Nazis had been issued with poison capsules. Seemingly, both men had used them to kill themselves.

Axmann succeeded for a time in remaining free. He escaped from Berlin to Mecklenburg in the Soviet zone and in December 1945 was arrested by the US Army Counter-Intelligence Corps when he ventured into Upper Bavaria. Denazification courts imposed a fine and a brief period of imprisonment. The general conclusion was that Axmann had become a Nazi out of ideological conviction and was not guilty of any criminal behaviour.

But by then the Third Reich had passed into history.

21

For 12th SS-Panzer Division Hitlerjugend the end came on 8 May 1945. But not before the division had fought its last, strictly personal battle in Austria. And won.

The tattered remnants of the division had trudged towards Linz to surrender to the Americans; no one, not even the most unrepentant fanatic, relished an end at the hands of the Russians.

At the town of Enns, Hugo Kraas, the division's last commander, swelled with pride as he took the dignified salute of the Hitler Youth.

A humiliating order had been given by the American captors; white flags of surrender were to be displayed. The division, in a last act of bravado, ignored the instruction. A mere 455 men and one tank, all that was left of one of Germany's foremost armoured divisions, then went into captivity with full soldierly bearing.

For the former SS-Oberfuehrer Kurt Meyer, 29 December 1945 was the most bizarre thirty-fifth birthday imaginable.

Here he was, a prisoner of the Canadians, being ordered out of his makeshift cell in the former naval signals school outside the East Frisian town of Aurich. The actions of his guards were puzzling; he was escorted to the washroom, ordered to strip and take a bath. Then, still under solemn escort, he found himself in another room where the scene was so incredible that he felt sure the whole thing was a dream. There was a table groaning with food and drink. Furthermore, standing by it were some half a dozen Canadian officers grinning at his bewilderment.

Some of 'Panzer' Meyer's former enemies, men of the Canadian 3rd Infantry Division, respected the man they regarded as an honourable opponent; they had laid on a surprise birthday celebration for him.

In fact, Meyer had precious little time to celebrate. For he downed his birthday drinks almost literally under the shadow of the hangman's noose.

After surrendering to the Belgian farmer and his young son, Meyer had been sent to England as a rather special prisoner. He was held at the so-called London District Cage, the Kensington headquarters of the War Crimes Investigation Unit. The Schutzstaffel had been designated a criminal organisation; there could, it was felt, be grounds for prosecution against 'Panzer' Meyer.

There were.

If it had not been for the emergence of seventeen-year-old former SS-Sturmmann Jan Jesionek, Meyer might have been able to endure his imprisonment with some equanimity. But Jesionek, captured and interrogated by the Americans, had an interesting story.

He had been a conscript with the 15th Reconnaissance Company of the 25th SS-Panzer Grenadier Regiment, and had been wounded at Bretteville on the night of 8/9 June 1944. After three months in hospital, he had been sent to a replacement unit – and had promptly deserted to the Americans.

During interrogation at Chartres, he said that on the morning of 8 June he had brought prisoners to the command post of the regiment, located between Caen and Bretteville.

Jesionek had found himself facing 'Panzer' Meyer.

The latter had been in a foul mood and shouted: 'Why do you bring prisoners to the rear? The murderers do nothing but eat our rations.'

Then he had turned to another officer and barked: 'In future I don't want any prisoners brought here.'

To his considerable relief, Jesionek was then able to withdraw. As he crossed the courtyard after leaving Meyer, he spotted a pump and decided on a quick wash. What he saw next had rooted him to the spot.

The Canadian prisoners were marched past him, through what appeared to be an opening to a small park or garden. As they reached the opening, each was shot in the back of the head by an SS-Unterscharfuehrer.

The killings over, Jesionek had wandered across and stared at the bodies. Next, his interrogators made him draw a detailed map of the area where the shootings had taken place. Then the questioning had got tougher. Over days, Jesionek was made to repeat his story constantly. His testimony, in essential details, did not change.

After that, it was the turn of French occupants of nearby buildings. They were able to reveal that, only a few weeks before, something had been observed in the garden protruding from the ground. The Canadian graves officer in the district had been notified.

Eventually, eighteen bodies of Canadian soldiers were discovered in five different graves.

The questioning then switched to Kurt Meyer in London. It was conducted for the most part by a formidable inquisitor, Colonel Alexander Scotland. The latter's verdict on Meyer was succinct: 'A bully of a commander . . . His was the voice which in the beer garden always rose above everyone else's. I had met many such. Nor was it difficult to imagine how it was that the aggressive Meyer, active, self-possessed . . . had so rapidly advanced from the rank of Captain to Lieutenant-General in the space of a few years.'

Previously, Meyer's questioners had not spoken German and had relied heavily on interpreters. The wily Meyer, who knew far more English than he let on, was able to turn the situation to his advantage. There was welcome breathing space to think up his answers.

All that was in the past now. The Englishman spoke perfect German. Any attempt at evasion had Scotland barking: 'Come on, Meyer, let's hear it, and no non-sense.' A stumbling reply was invariably greeted with: 'Out with it, Meyer; you know exactly what I'm getting at.'

All of which is why, on a foggy morning in November 1945, a handcuffed 'Panzer' Meyer landed back in Germany aboard a military transport aircraft and had to face shouting, pushing press and cameramen.

Meyer correctly saluted the knot of Canadians who were there to meet him. The gesture was ignored; the prisoner was hustled to a waiting car.

Within hours, a colonel of the 4th Winnipeg Rifles was informing him of the reason for his sudden arrival back in Germany. He was to be tried as a war criminal and the charges were:

1. In Belgium in 1943 and in France in 1944, as a commander of the 25th SS-Panzer Grenadier Regiment, he had ordered the troops under his command to show no mercy to Allied troops.
2. That he, Meyer, had committed a war crime in Normandy in that as Commander of the 25th SS-Panzer Grenadier Regiment he was responsible for the murder of seven Canadian prisoners near his HQ.

The assembled evidence looked damning against 'Panzer' Meyer. Captain Percy Bell of the Canadian Graves Unit reported that the bodies exhumed at the military cemetery to which they had been moved, in each case, showed death had been due to head wounds.

These had come either from bullets or from a blunt instrument such as a club or a rifle butt.

From the outset, Meyer denied any knowledge whatever of the killing of prisoners. The interrogators probed deeper. *All* prisoners? Uncomfortably, Meyer shifted his ground. Well, not *quite* all prisoners. He had served in Russia and there had been cases of executions there. Among themselves, the interrogators expressed satisfaction. Confession, they knew, was addictive; get a man to concede one point and he will often go on to admit others, usually through pure fatigue.

For a time it did not look as if this would work with Kurt Meyer. He yielded not one inch on the question of the murders at Abbaye Ardenne.

Then came a dramatic change of heart. Meyer announced: 'I want to make a new statement.' The interrogators were scrupulously fair; Meyer was advised to wait until the trial; after all, not even a defence counsel had been appointed.

But now there was no holding Kurt Meyer. He asked for a transcript of early interrogations. One passage bothered him particularly:

'Was it reported to you by anyone that Allied prisoners had died at your headquarters and that it was necessary to bury them there?'
'No.'

But now Meyer was saying: 'The point raised is not one hundred per cent correct and I do not want to be regarded as a perjurer at the trial.'

In other words, the time had come to tell the truth – or something far nearer to it.

Now Meyer was saying that two officers had reported to him that they had found unburied bodies of Canadians who had been shot in the area of Abbaye Ardenne.

Meyer recalled: 'I sent my adjutant, Oberscharfuehrer Schueman, to investigate. He confirmed the report and I went over myself to make the inspection. All the Canadians had been shot through the head. I then reported the matter to my divisional commander, SS-Brigadefuehrer Witt, who was very angry and asked me to discover who was responsible.'

Meyer had then, he claimed, ordered the prisoners to be buried and an investigation to be carried out. But then had come Witt's death and the promotion of Meyer to divisional commander. Nothing had been done.

The drawback to Meyer's statement was that none of it could be proved. All the witnesses were long dead; no one felt inclined to believe 'Panzer' Meyer.

Five days after that astonishing birthday party, the court had its final session. In flat, unemotional tones the verdict was read out:

'Kurt Meyer, this Court has found you guilty on three counts. You are sentenced to death by shooting. This Court is now closed.'

Meyer stood rigidly to attention as the verdict was read out. Clenched teeth and a grim expression revealed the only emotion. Then he bowed slightly, swung around and marched out of the court without a word.

But there were those who felt that the verdict was unjust, that there was no clear evidence that Meyer had ordered the shooting of the Canadian prisoners. Among the Canadians he had some ardent champions. Indeed the authorities were uneasy; the first stage was the commutation of 'Panzer' Meyer's sentence to life imprisonment. Then, in 1951, Meyer was sent back to Germany from a Canadian prison. On 7 September 1954 he was finally released after serving ten years in jail. For the remainder of his life, he devoted his time to the welfare of former SS men through HIAG, the Waffen-SS Old Comrades' Association.

A change of heart by now certainly seemed genuine. Meyer urged that HIAG should be entirely an ex-servicemen's organisation and should have no associations with neo-Nazi groups. On 23 December 1961, the former SS-Oberfuehrer Kurt Meyer died in his bed.

For Baldur von Schirach there remained the balm of memory; in the face of a twenty-year sentence at Nuremberg, neither the present nor the future offered much. Schirach was the man who had written many of the songs for the storm-troop marches of the 1930s, the leader who had gained the allegiance and the loyalty of the brown-shirted Hitler Youth and of the girls of the Bund Deutscher Maedchen in their uniform of white blouses and blue skirts. At a mere twenty-nine, he had been inside the Nazi hierarchy, reporting directly to the Fuehrer on behalf of *ten million* within Nazi Germany!

It had meant exercising power in conditions of extreme comfort. In Vienna, Schirach had ruled lavishly as Governor and Gauleiter. And there had been the adulation, particularly flattering when it came from the girls.

With the collapse of Nazi Germany, Schirach had melted away in the general chaos of a shattered Europe. Since he spoke faultless English, he was able to adopt the name Richard Falk and, sprouting a beard, work for a time as an interpreter at an American post. But for prominent ex-Nazis the heat was on.

He decided on a bold gamble, presenting himself to the Americans and saying simply: 'I am Schirach.' He reasoned that his strong American family background would count for something, particularly if he showed due repentance.

Schirach worked hard at repentance. His confession before the International Military Tribunal stated: 'It is my guilt that I educated youth for a man who committed a millionfold murders; I carry the guilt for youth reared in an anti-Semitic state under anti-Semitic laws . . .'

On the orders of General Patton, he had sent a message to surviving youth of the former Nazi Germany, telling them that there should be no underground movement, no myth to perpetuate the memory of Adolf Hitler and no anti-Semitism.

The judges at Nuremberg were not impressed. Indeed, there were signs that Schirach's repentance did not stand close examination. In 1948, from his cell at Spandau jail, he had written to Henriette: 'We did not realise the luck that belonged to us.'

Humiliation and misery were largely to dog Schirach throughout his time in Spandau. The man who had wallowed in luxury and lived in such splendour in Austria with a retinue of seventeen servants was forced to mop the gymnasium in the Nuremberg prison, following the hanging of ten leading Nazis. The man who even in the dock dressed in a smart dove-grey suit as if about to set out for a stroll down the Kurfuerstendamm was put to basket-weaving and tending the prison garden.

Then, five years into his sentence, came the hardest blow of all. Henriette wrote a letter to her husband which concluded: 'I intend to divorce you immediately.'

Henriette had grumbled constantly over the years that the Nazi party and his faith in Adolf Hitler had come well before family considerations.

And now, for the following fifteen years of his sentence, Baldur von Schirach, the prime architect of Hitler Youth, had at last to face facts; all his worlds had finally been destroyed.

SELECTED BIBLIOGRAPHY

Bauer, Lt. Col. E., *The History of World War II* (Galahad Books, New York, 1966)

Burden, H.T., *The Nuremberg Party Rallies, 1923–1939* (Pall Mall Press, London, 1967)

Butler, Rupert, *The Black Angels* (Arrow, 1978)

Cooper, Matthew, *The German Air Force 1933–1945: An Anatomy of a Failure* (Jane's, 1981)

Cowan, Lore, *Children of the Resistance* (Leslie Frewin, 1968)

Cross, Robin, *V.E. Day* (Sidgwick & Jackson, 1985)

Fishman, Jack, *Long Knives and Short Memories: The Spandau Prison Story* (Souvenir Press, 1986)

Goolrick, William K. & Tanner, Ogden, *The Battle of the Bulge* (Time-Life Books, 1979)

* Hagen, Louis, *Follow My Leader* (Allan Wingate, 1951)

Kessler, Leo, *The Iron Fist: A History of the SS-Panzer Divisions* (Futura Publications, 1977)

Koch, H.W., *The Hitler Youth: Origins and Development 1922–1945* (Macdonald & Jane's, 1975)

* Koehn, Ilse, *Mischling, Second Degree: My Childhood in Nazi Germany* (Hamish Hamilton, 1977)

Lucas, James & Cooper, Matthew, *Hitler's Elite Leibstandarte-SS* (Macdonald & Jane's, 1975)

Macdonald, Charles B., *The Battle of the Bulge* (Weidenfeld & Nicolson, 1984)

McKee, Alexander, *Caen: Anvil of Victory* (Macmillan, 1964)

* Maschmann, M., *Fazit* (Deutsches Verlags-Anstalt,

Stuttgart, 1964)

Maule, Henry, *Caen* (David & Charles, 1976)

O'Donnell, James P., *The Berlin Bunker* (J.M. Dent & Sons, 1979)

* Pallud, Jean Paul, *Battle of the Bulge: Then and Now* (After the Battle Magazine, 1984)

Prittie, Terence, *Germans Against Hitler* (Hutchinson, 1964)

Quarrie, Bruce, *Hitler's Samurai* (Patrick Stephens, 1983)

Reitlinger, Gerald, *The SS: Alibi of a Nation* (William Heinemann, 1956)

Shirer, William, *The Rise and Fall of the Third Reich* (Martin Secker & Warburg, 1960)

Shulman, Milton, *Defeat in the West* (Martin Secker & Warburg, 1947)

Theilen, Fritz, *Edelweiss Piraten* (Fischer Taschenbuch Verlag, 1984)

Tolland, John, *Adolf Hitler* (Doubleday & Co., 1976)

Trevor-Roper, H.R., *The Last Days of Hitler* (revised edition) (Macmillan, 1972)

Von Schirach, Henriette, *The Price of Glory* (Frederick Muller, 1960)

Wheeler-Bennett, John W., *The Nemesis of Power* (Macmillan, 1961)

Whiting, Charles, *The Battle of the Ruhr Pocket* (Pan, 1970)

Whiting, Charles, *The Home Front: Germany* (Time-Life Books, 1982)

Ziemke, Earl F., *The Battle for Berlin: End of the Third Reich* (Macdonald, 1969)

* The author would like to thank the publishers for permission to use quoted material.

BESTSELLING NON-FICTION FROM ARROW

All these books are available from your bookshop or news-agent or you can order them direct. Just tick the titles you want and complete the form below.

☐	THE GREAT ESCAPE	Paul Brickhill	£1.75
☐	A RUMOR OF WAR	Philip Caputo	£2.50
☐	A LITTLE ZIT ON THE SIDE	Jasper Carrott	£1.50
☐	THE ART OF COARSE ACTING	Michael Green	£1.50
☐	THE UNLUCKIEST MAN IN THE WORLD	Mike Harding	£1.75
☐	DIARY OF A SOMEBODY	Christopher Matthew	£1.25
☐	TALES FROM A LONG ROOM	Peter Tinniswood	£1.75
☐	LOVE WITHOUT FEAR	Eustace Chesser	£1.95
☐	NO CHANGE	Wendy Cooper	£1.95
☐	MEN IN LOVE	Nancy Friday	£2.75

Postage

Total

ARROW BOOKS, BOOKSERVICE BY POST, PO BOX 29, DOUGLAS, ISLE OF MAN, BRITISH ISLES

Please enclose a cheque or postal order made out to Arrow Books Ltd for the amount due including 15p per book for postage and packing both for orders within the UK and for overseas orders.

Please print clearly

NAME ....

ADDRESS ....

....

Whilst every effort is made to keep prices down and to keep popular books in print, Arrow Books cannot guarantee that prices will be the same as those advertised here or that the books will be available.